WAR

WAR

BY
PIERRE LOTI

TRANSLATED FROM THE FRENCH BY
MARJORIE LAURIE

PHILADELPHIA AND LONDON
J. B. LIPPINCOTT COMPANY
1917

COPYRIGHT, 1917, BY J. B. LIPPINCOTT COMPANY

Printed by J. B. Lippincott Company
The Washington Square Press, Philadelphia, U. S. A.

TO MY FRIEND
LOUIS BARTHOU, P.L.

CONTENTS

		PAGE
I.	A Letter to the Minister of Marine	9
II.	Two Poor Little Nestlings of Belgium	12
III.	A Gay Little Scene at the Battle Front	18
IV.	Letter to Enver Pasha	28
V.	Another Scene at the Battle Front	34
VI.	The Phantom Basilica	53
VII.	The Flag Which Our Naval Brigade do not Yet Possess	68
VIII.	Tahiti and the Savages with Pink Skins Like Boiled Pig	80
IX.	A Little Hussar	85
X.	An Evening at Ypres	95
XI.	At the General Headquarters of the Belgian Army	111
XII.	Some Words Uttered by Her Majesty, the Queen of the Belgians	127
XIII.	An Appeal on Behalf of the Seriously Wounded in the East	139
XIV.	Serbia in the Balkan War	148
XV.	Above All Let Us Never Forget!	151
XVI.	The Inn of the Good Samaritan	157

CONTENTS

XVII.	For the Rescue of Our Wounded..	174
XVIII.	At Rheims.......................	177
XIX.	The Death-Bearing Gas...........	192
XX.	All-Souls' Day with the Armies at the Front.................	205
XXI.	The Cross of Honour for the Flag of the Naval Brigade...........	211
XXII.	The Absent-Minded Pilgrim.......	219
XXIII.	The First Sunshine of March.....	242
XXIV.	At Soissons.....................	265
XXV.	The Two Gorgon Heads...........	299

WAR
I
A LETTER TO THE MINISTER OF MARINE

Captain J. Viaud of the Naval Reserve, to the Minister of Marine.

Rochefort, August 18th, 1914.

Sir,

When I was recalled to active service on the outbreak of war I had hopes of performing some duty less insignificant than that which was assigned to me in our dockyards.

Believe me, I have no reproaches to make, for I am very well aware that the Navy will not fill the principal rôle in this war, and that all my comrades of the same rank are likewise destined to almost complete inaction for mere lack of opportunity, like myself doomed, alas! to see their energies sapped, their spirits in torment.

But let me invoke the other name I bear. The average man is not as a rule well versed in Naval Regulations. Will it not, then, be a bad example in our dear country, where everyone is doing his duty so splendidly, if Pierre Loti is to serve no useful end? The exercise of two professions places me as an officer in a somewhat exceptional position, does it not? Forgive me then for soliciting a degree of exceptional and indulgent treatment. I should accept with joy, with pride, any position whatsoever that would bring me nearer to the fighting-line, even if it were a very subordinate post, one much below the dignity of my five rows of gold braid.

Or, on the other hand, in the last resort, could I not be appointed a supernumerary on special duty on some ship which might have a chance of seeing real fighting? I assure you that I should find some means of making myself useful there. Or, finally, if there are too many rules and regulations in the way, would you grant me, sir, while waiting until my services may be required by the Fleet, liberty to come and go, so that I may try to find some kind of employment, even if it be only ambulance work? My lot is hard, and no one will understand that the mere fact that I am a captain in the Naval Reserve dooms me to almost complete inaction, while all France is in arms.

(*Signed*) JULIEN VIAUD.
(PIERRE LOTI.)

II
TWO POOR LITTLE NESTLINGS OF BELGIUM

August, 1914.

One evening a train full of Belgian refugees had just entered the railway station of one of our southern towns. Worn out and dazed, the poor martyrs stepped down slowly, one by one, on to the unfamiliar platform where Frenchmen were waiting to welcome them. Carrying with them a few articles of clothing, caught up at haphazard, they had climbed up into the coaches without so much as asking themselves what was their destination. They had taken refuge there in hurried flight, desperate flight from horror and death, from fire, mutilations unspeakable and Sadic outrages—such things, deemed no longer possible on earth, had been brooding still, it seemed, in the depths of pietistic German brains, and, like an ultimate spewing forth of primeval barbarities, had burst suddenly upon their country and upon our own. Village, hearth, family— nothing remained to them; without purpose, like waifs and strays, they had drifted there, and in the eyes of all lay horror and anguish. Among them were many children, little girls, whose parents were lost in the midst of conflagrations or battles; aged grandmothers, too, now alone in the world, who had fled, scarce knowing why, clinging no longer to life, yet urged on by some obscure instinct of self-preservation. The faces of these aged women expressed no emotion, not even despair; it seemed as if their souls had actually abandoned their bodies and reason their brains.

Lost in that mournful throng were two quite young children, holding each other tightly by the hand, two little boys, evidently two little brothers. The elder, five years of age perhaps, was protecting the younger, whose age may have been three. No one claimed them; no one knew them. When they found themselves alone, how was it that they understood that if they would escape death they, too, must climb into that train? Their clothes were neat, and they wore warm little woollen stockings. Evidently they belonged to humble but careful parents. Doubtless they were the sons of one of those glorious soldiers of Belgium who fell like heroes upon the field of honour—sons of a father who, in the moment of death, must needs have bestowed upon them one last and tender thought. So overwhelmed were they with weariness and want of sleep that they did not even cry. Scarcely could they stand upright. They could not answer the questions that were put to them, but above all they refused to let go of each other; that they would not do. At last the big, elder brother, still gripping the other's hand for fear of losing him, realised the responsibilities of his character of protector; he summoned up strength to speak to the lady with the brassard, who was bending down to him.

"Madame," he said, in a very small, beseeching voice, already half-asleep, "Madame, is anyone going to put us to bed?"

For the moment this was the only wish they were capable of forming; all that they looked for from the mercy of mankind was that someone would be so good as to put them to bed. They were soon put to bed, together, you may be sure, and they went to sleep at once, still holding hands and nestling close to each other, both sinking in the same instant into the peaceful oblivion of children's slumbers.

One day long ago, in the China Seas during the war, two bewildered little birds, two tiny little birds, smaller even than our wren, had made their way, I know not how, on board our iron-clad and into our admiral's quarters. No one, to be sure, had sought to frighten them, and all day long they had fluttered about from side to side, perching on cornices or on green plants. By nightfall I had forgotten them, when the admiral sent for me. It was to show me, with emotion, his two little visitors; they had gone to sleep in his room, perched on one leg upon a silken cord fastened above his bed. Like two little balls of feathers, touching and almost mingling in one, they slept close, very close together, without the slightest fear, as if very sure of our pity.

And these poor little Belgian children, sleeping side by side, made me think of those two nestlings, astray in the midst of the China Seas. Theirs, too, was the same trust; theirs the same innocent slumber. But these children were to be protected with a far more tender solicitude.

III

A GAY LITTLE SCENE AT THE BATTLE FRONT

October, 1914.

At about eleven o'clock in the morning of that day I arrived at a village—its name I have, let us say, forgotten. My companion was an English commandant, whom the fortunes of war had given me for comrade since the previous evening. Our path was lighted by that great and genial magician, the sun—a radiant sun, a holiday sun, transfiguring and beautifying all things. This occurred in a department in the extreme north of France, which one it was I have never known, but the weather was so fine that we might have imagined ourselves in Provence.

For nearly two hours our way lay

hemmed in between two columns of soldiers, marching in opposite directions. On our right were the English going into action, very clean, very fresh, with an air of satisfaction and in high spirits. They were admirably equipped and their horses in the pink of condition. On our left were French Artillerymen coming back from the Titanic battle to enjoy a little rest. The latter were coated with dust, and some wore bandages round arm and forehead, but they still preserved their gaiety of countenance and the aspect of healthy men, and they marched in sections in good order. They were actually bringing back quantities of empty cartridge cases, which they had found time to collect, a sure proof that they had withdrawn from the scene of action at their leisure, unhurried and unafraid—victorious soldiers to whom their chiefs had prescribed a few days' respite. In the distance we heard a noise like a thunderstorm, muffled at first, to which we were drawing nearer and yet nearer. Peasants were working in the adjoining fields as if nothing unusual were happening, and yet they were not sure that the savages, who were responsible for such tumult yonder, would not come back one of these days and pillage everything. Here and there in the meadows, on the grass, sat groups of fugitives, clustered around little wood fires. The scene would have been dismal enough on a gloomy day, but the sun managed to shed a cheerful light upon it. They cooked their meals in gipsy fashion, surrounded by bundles in which they had hurriedly packed together their scanty clothing in the terrible rush for safety.

Our motor car was filled with packets of cigarettes and with newspapers, which kind souls had commissioned us to carry to the men in the firing-line, and so slow was our progress, so closely were we hemmed in by the two columns of soldiers, that we were able to distribute our gifts through the doors of the car, to the English on our right, to the French on our left. They stretched out their hands to catch them in mid-air, and thanked us with a smile and a quick salute.

There were also villagers who travelled along that overcrowded road mingling in confusion with the soldiers. I remember a very pretty young peasant woman, who was dragging along by a string, in the midst of the English transport wagons, a little go-cart with two sleeping babies. She was toiling along, for the gradient just there was steep. A handsome Scotch sergeant, with a golden moustache, who sat on the back of the nearest wagon smoking a cigarette and dangling his legs, beckoned to her.

"Give me the end of your string."

She understood and accepted his offer with a smile of pretty confusion. The Scotchman wound the fragile tow-rope round his left arm, keeping his right arm free so that he might go on smoking. So it was really he who brought along these two babies of France, while the heavy transport lorry drew their little cart like a feather.

When we entered the village, the sun shone with increasing splendour. Such chaos, such confusion prevailed there as had never been seen before, and after this war, unparalleled in history, will never again be witnessed. Uniforms of every description, weapons of every sort, Scots, French cuirassiers, Turcos, Zouaves, Bedouins, whose burnouses swung upwards with a noble gesture as they saluted. The church square was blocked with huge English motor-omnibuses that had once been a means of communication in the streets of London, and still displayed in large letters the names of certain districts of that city. I shall be accused of exaggeration, but it is a fact that these omnibuses wore a look of astonishment at finding themselves rolling along, packed with soldiers, over the soil of France.

All these people, mingled together in confusion, were making preparations for luncheon. Those savages yonder (who might perhaps arrive here on the morrow —who could say?) still conducted their great symphony, their incessant cannonade, but no one paid any attention to it. Who, moreover, could be uneasy in such beautiful surroundings, such surprising autumn sunshine, while roses still grew on the walls, and many-coloured dahlias in gardens that the white frost had scarcely touched? Everyone settled down to the meal and made the best of things. You would have thought you were looking at a festival, a somewhat incongruous and unusual festival, to be sure, improvised in the vicinity of some tower of Babel. Girls wandered about among the groups; little fair-haired children gave away fruit they had gathered in their own orchards. Scotsmen in shirt-sleeves were persuaded that the country they were in was warm by comparison with their own. Priests and Red Cross sisters were finding seats for the wounded on packing-cases. One good old sister, with a face like parchment, and frank, pretty eyes under her mob-cap, took infinite pains to make a Zouave comfortable, whose arms were both wrapped in bandages. Doubtless she would presently feed him as if he were a little child.

We ourselves, the Englishman and I, were very hungry, so we made our way to the pleasant-looking inn, where officers were already seated at table with soldiers of lower rank. (In these times of torment in which we live hierarchal barriers no longer exist.)

"I could certainly give you roast beef and rabbit *sauté*," said the innkeeper, "but as for bread, no indeed! it is not to be had; you cannot buy bread anywhere at any price."

"Ah!" said my comrade, the English commandant, "and what about those excellent loaves over there standing up against the door?"

"Oh, those loaves belong to a general who sent them here, because he is coming to luncheon with his aides-de-camp."

Hardly had he turned his back when my companion hastily drew a knife from his pocket, sliced off the end of one of those golden loaves, and hid it under his coat.

"We have found some bread," he said calmly to the innkeeper, "so you can bring luncheon."

So, seated beside an Arab officer of *la*

Grande Tente, dressed in a red burnous, we luncheon gaily with our guests, the soldier-chauffeurs of our motor car.

When we left the inn to continue our journey the festival of the sun was at its height; it cast a glad light upon that ill-assorted throng and the strange motor-omnibuses. A convoy of German prisoners was crossing the square; bestial and sly of countenance they marched between our own soldiers, who kept time infinitely better than they; scarcely a glance was thrown at them.

The old nun I spoke of, so old and so pure-eyed, was helping her Zouave to smoke a cigarette, holding it to his lips rather awkwardly with trembling, grandmotherly solicitude. At the same time she seemed to be telling him some quite amusing stories—with the innocent, ingenuous merriment of which good nuns have the secret—for they were both laughing. Who can say what little childish tale it may have been? An old parish priest, who was smoking his pipe near them—without any particular refinement, I am bound to admit —laughed, too, to see them laugh. And just as we were going into our car to continue our journey to those regions of horror where the cannon were thundering, a little girl of twelve ran and plucked a sheaf of autumn asters from her garden to deck us with flowers.

What good people there are still in the world! And how greatly has the aggression of German savages reinforced those tender bonds of brotherhood that unite all who are truly of the human species.

IV
LETTER TO ENVER PASHA

Rochefort, September 4th, 1914.

My Dear and Great Friend,

Forgive my letter for the sake of my affection and admiration for yourself and of my regard for your country, which to some extent I have made my own. In the country round Tripoli you played the part of splendid hero, without fear and without reproach, holding your own, ten men against a thousand. In Thrace it was you who recovered Adrianople for Turkey, and this feat, the recapture of that town of heroes, you effected almost without bloodshed. Everywhere, with the violence necessitated by the circumstances, you suppressed cruelty and brigandage. I witnessed your indignation against the atrocities of the Bulgarians, and you yourself desired me to visit, in your service motor car, the ruins of those villages through which the assassins had passed.

Well, I will tell you a fact of which you are doubtless yet ignorant: In Belgium, in France, and moreover *by order,* the Germans are committing these same abominations which the Bulgarians committed in your country, and they are a thousand times more detestable still, for the Bulgarians were primitive mountaineers under the influence of fanaticism, whereas these others are civilised. Civilised? So fundamental is their brutality that culture has no grasp of their souls and nothing can be expected of them.

Turkey to-day desires to win back her islands; this point no one who is not blinded with prejudice can fail to understand. But I tremble lest she should go too far in this war. Alas! well do I divine the pressure that is brought to bear upon your dear country and yourself by that execrable being, the incarnation of all the vices of the Prussian race, ferocity, arrogance, and trickery. Doubtless he has seen good to take advantage of your fine and ardent patriotism, luring you on with illusive promises of revenge. Beware of his lies! Assuredly he has contrived to keep truth from reaching you, else would he have alienated your loyal soldier's heart. Even as he has convinced a section of his own people, so he has known how to persuade you that these butcheries were forced upon him. It is not so; they were planned long ago with devilish cynicism. He has succeeded in inspiring you with faith in his victories, though he knows, as to-day the whole world knows, that in the end the triumph will rest with us. And even if by some impossible chance we were to succumb for a time, neverthless would Prussia and her dynasty of tigerish brutes remain nailed fast forever to the most shameful pillory in all the history of mankind.

How deeply should I suffer were I to see our dear Turkey, by this wretch, hurl herself in his train into a terrible venture. More painful still were it to witness her dishonour, should she associate herself with these ultimate barbarians in their attack upon civilisation. Oh, could you but know with what infinite loathing the whole world looks upon the Prussian race!

Alas! you owe no debt to France, that I know only too well. We lent our authority to Italy's attempt upon Tripoli. Later, in the beginning of the Balkan War, we forgot the age-long hospitality so generously offered to us Frenchmen, to our seminaries, to our culture, to our language, which you have almost made your own. In thoughtlessness and ignorance we sided with your neighbours, from whom our nation received naught but ill-will and persecution. We initiated against you a campaign of calumny, and only too late we have acknowledged its injustice. The Germans, on the other hand, were alone in affording you a little—oh, a very little!—encouragement. But even so, it is not worth your committing suicide for their sakes. Moreover, you see, in this very hour, these people are succeeding in putting themselves outside the pale of humanity. To march in their company would become not only a danger, but a degradation.

Your influence over your country is fully justified; may you hold her back on that fatal decline to which she seems committed. My letter will be long on the way, but when it arrives your eyes may perhaps be already opened, despite the web of lies in which Germany has entrammelled you.

Forgive me if I wish to be of the number of those by whose means some hint of the truth may reach you.

I maintain an unwavering faith in our final triumph, but on the day of our deliverance how would my joy be veiled in mourning if my second country, my country of the Orient, were to bury itself under the débris of the hideous Empire of Prussia.

V

ANOTHER SCENE AT THE BATTLE FRONT

October, 1914.

Whereabouts, you may ask, did this come to pass? Well, it is one of the peculiarities of this war, that in spite of my familiarity with maps, and notwithstanding the excellence in detail of the plans which I carry about with me, I never know where I am. At any rate this certainly happened somewhere. I have, moreover, a sad conviction that it happened in France. I should so much have preferred it to have happened in Germany, for it was close up to the enemy's lines, under fire of their guns.

I had travelled by motor car since morning, and had passed through more towns, large and small, than I can count. I re-

WAR 35

member one scene in a village where I halted, a village which had certainly never before seen motor-omnibuses or throngs of soldiers and horses. Some fifty German prisoners were brought in. They were unshaven, unshorn, and highly unprepossessing. I will not flatter them by saying that they looked like savages, for true savages in the bush are seldom lacking either in distinction or grace of bearing. Such air as these Germans had was a blackguard air of doltish ugliness—dull, gross, incurable.

A pretty girl of somewhat doubtful character, with feathers in her hat, who had taken up a position there to watch them go past, stared at them with ill-concealed resentment.

" Oh indeed, is it with freaks like those that their dirty Kaiser invites us to breed for beauty? God's truth!" and she clinched her unfinished phrase by spitting on the ground.

For the next hour or two I passed through a deserted countryside, woods in autumn colouring and leafless forests which seemed interminable under a gloomy sky. It was cold, with that bitter, penetrating chill which we hardly know in my home in south-west France, and which seemed characteristic of northern lands.

From time to time a village through which the barbarians had passed displayed to us its ruins, charred and blackened by fire. Here and there by the wayside lay little grave-mounds, either singly or grouped together—mounds lately dug; a few leaves had been scattered above them and a cross made of two sticks. Soldiers, their names now for ever forgotten, had fallen there exhausted and had breathed their last with none to help them.

We scarcely noticed them, for we raced along with ever-increasing speed, because the night of late October was already closing rapidly in upon us. As the day advanced a mist almost wintry in character thickened around us like a shroud. Silence pervaded with still deeper melancholy all that countryside, which, although the barbarians had been expelled from it, still had memories of all those butcheries, ravings, outcries, and conflagrations.

In the midst of a forest, near a hamlet, of which nothing remained save fragments of calcined walls, there were two graves lying side by side. Near these I halted to look at a little girl of twelve years, quite alone there, arranging bunches of flowers sprinkled with water, some poor chrysanthemums from her ruined plot of garden, some wild flowers too, the last scabious of the season, gathered in that place of mourning.

"Were they friends of yours, my child, those two who are sleeping there?"

"Oh no, sir, but I know that they were Frenchmen; I saw them being buried. They were young, sir, and their moustaches were scarcely grown."

There was no inscription on these crosses, soon to be blown down by winter winds and to crumble away in the grass. Who were they? Sons of peasants, of simple citizens, of aristocrats? Who weeps for them? Is it a mother in skilfully fashioned draperies of crape? Is it a mother in the homely weeds of a peasant woman? Whichever it be, those who loved them will live and die without ever knowing that they lie mouldering there by the side of a lonely road on the northern boundary of France; without ever knowing that this kind little girl, whose own home lay desolate, brought them an offering of flowers one autumn evening, while with the advent of night a bitter cold was descending upon the forest which wrapped them round.

Farther on I came to a village, the headquarters of a general officer in command of an army corps. Here an officer joined me in my motor car, who undertook to guide me to one particular point of the vast battle front.

We drove on rapidly for another hour through a country without inhabitants. In the meantime we passed one of these long convoys of what were once motor-omnibuses in Paris, but have been converted since the war into slaughter-houses on wheels. Townspeople, men and women, sat there once, where now sides of beef, all red and raw, swing suspended from hooks. If we did not know that in those fields yonder there were hundreds of thousands of men to be fed we might well ask why such things were being carted in the midst of this deserted country through which we are hastening at top speed.

The day is waning rapidly, and a continuous rumbling of a storm begins to make itself heard, unchained seemingly on a level with the earth. For weeks now this same storm has thundered away without pause along a sinuous line stretching across France from east to west, a line on which daily, alas! new heaps of dead are piled up.

"Here we are," said my guide.

If I were not already familiar with the new characteristics wherewith the Germans have endued a battle front, I should believe, in spite of the incessant cannonade, that he had made a mistake, for at first sight there is no sign either of army or of soldiers. We are in a place of sinister aspect, a vast plain; the greyish ground is stripped of its turf and torn up; trees here and there are shattered more or less completely, as if by some cataclysm of thunderbolts or hailstones. There is no trace of human existence, not even the ruins of a village; nothing characteristic of any period, either of historical or even of geological development. Gazing into the distance at the far-flung forest skyline fading on all sides into the darkening mists of twilight, we might well believe ourselves to have reverted to a prehistoric epoch of the world's history.

"Here we are."

That means that it is time to hide our motor car under some trees or it will attract a rain of shells and endanger the lives of our chauffeurs, for in that misty forest opposite there are many wicked eyes watching us through wonderful binoculars, by whose aid they are as keen of sight as great birds of prey. To reach the firing-line, then, it is incumbent on us to proceed on foot.

How strange the ground looks! It is riddled with shell-holes, resembling enormous craters; in another place it is scarred and pierced and sown with pointed bullets, copper cartridge-cases, fragments of spiked helmets, and barbarian filth of other sorts. But in spite of its deserted appearance, this region is nevertheless thickly populated, only the inhabitants are no doubt troglodytes, for their dwellings, scattered about and invisible at first sight, are a kind of cave or molehill, half covered with branches and leaves. I had seen the same kind of architecture once upon a time on Easter Island, and the sight of these dwellings of men in this scenery of primeval forest completes our earlier impression of having leapt backwards into the abyss of time.

Of a truth, to force upon us such a reversion was a right Prussian artifice. War, which was once a gallant affair of parades in the sunshine, of beautiful uniforms and of music, war they have rendered a mean and ugly thing. They wage it like burrowing beasts, and obviously there was nothing left for us but to imitate them.

In the meantime here and there heads look out from the excavations to see who is coming. There is nothing prehistoric about these heads, any more than there is about the service-caps they are wearing; these are the faces of our own soldiers, with an air of health and good humour and of amusement at having to live there like rabbits. A sergeant comes up to us; he is as earthy as a mole that has not had time to clean itself, but he has a merry look of youth and gaiety.

"Take two or three men with you," I say to him, "and go and unpack my motor car, down there behind the trees. You will find a thousand packets of cigarettes and some picture-papers which some people in Paris have sent you to help to pass the time in the trenches.''

What a pity that I cannot take back and show, as a thanksgiving to the kind donors, the smiles of satisfaction with which their gifts were welcomed.

Another mile or two have still to be covered on foot before we reach the firing-line. An icy wind blows from the forests opposite that are yet more deeply drowned in black mists, forests in the enemy's hands, where the counterfeit thunderstorm is grumbling. This plain with its miserable molehills is a dismal place in the twilight, and I marvel that they can be so gay, these dear soldiers of ours, in the midst of the desolation surrounding them.

I cross this piece of ground, riddled with holes; the tempest of shot has spared here and there a tuft of grass, a little moss, a poor flower. The first place I reach is a line of defence in course of construction, which will be the second line of defence, to meet the improbable event of the first line, which lies farther ahead, having to be abandoned. Our soldiers are working like navvies with shovels and picks in their hands. They are all resolute and happy, anxious to finish their work, and it will be formidable indeed, surrounded as it is with most deadly ambushes. It was the Germans, I admit, whose scheming, evil brains devised this whole system of galleries and snares; but we, more subtle and alert than they, have, in a few days, equalled them, if we have not beaten them, at their own game.

A mile farther on is the first line. It is full of soldiers, for this is the trench that must withstand the shock of the barbarians' onset; day and night it is always ready to bristle with rifles, and they who hold the trench, gone to earth scarcely for a moment, know that they may expect at any minute the daily shower of shells. Then heads, rash enough to show themselves above the parapet, will be shot away, breasts shattered, entrails torn. They know, too, that they must be prepared to encounter at any unforeseen hour, in the pale sunlight or in the blackness of midnight, onslaughts of those barbarians with whom the forest opposite still swarms. They know how they will come on at a run, with shouts intended to terrify them, linked arm in arm into one infuriated mass, and how they will find means, as ever, to do much harm before death overtakes them entangled in our barbed wire. All this they know, for they have already seen it, but nevertheless they smile a serious, dignified smile. They have been nearly a week in this trench, waiting to be relieved, and they make no complaints.

"We are well fed," they say, "we eat

when we are hungry. As long as it does not rain we keep ourselves warm at night in our fox-holes with good thick blankets. But not all of us yet have woollen underclothing for the winter, and we shall need it soon. When you go back to Paris, Colonel, perhaps you will be so kind as to bring this to the notice of Government and of all the ladies too, who are working for us."

("Colonel"—the soldiers have no other title for officers with five rows of gold braid. On the last expedition to China I had already been called colonel, but I did not expect, alas! that I should be called so again during a war on the soil of France.)

These men who are talking to me at the edge of, or actually in, the trench belong to the most diverse social grades. Some were leisured dandies, some artisans, some day labourers, and there are even some who wear their caps at too rakish an angle and whose language smacks of the ring, into whose past it is better not to pry too curiously. Yet they have become not only good soldiers, but good men, for this war, while it has drawn us closer together, has at the same time purified us and ennobled us. This benefit at least the Germans will, involuntarily, have bestowed upon us, and indeed it is worth the trouble. Moreover our soldiers all know to-day why they are fighting, and therein lies their supreme strength. Their indignation will inspire them till their latest breath.

"When you have seen," said two young Breton peasants to me, "when you have seen with your own eyes what these brutes do in the villages they pass through, it is natural, is it not, to give your life to try to prevent them from doing as much in your own home?"

The cannonade roared an accompaniment in its deep, unceasing bass to this ingenuous statement.

Now this is the spirit that prevails inexhaustibly from one end of the fighting-line to the other. Everywhere there is the same determination and courage. Whether here or there, a talk with any of these soldiers is equally reassuring, and calls forth the same admiration.

But it is strange to reflect that in this twentieth century of ours, in order to protect ourselves from barbarism and horror, we have had to establish trenches such as these, in double and treble lines, crossing our dear country from east to west along an unbroken front of hundreds of miles, like a kind of Great Wall of China. But a hundred times more formidable than the original wall, the defence of the Mongolians, is this wall of ours, a wall practically subterranean, which winds along stealthily, manned by all the heroic youth of France, ever on the alert, ever in the midst of bloodshed.

The twilight this evening, under the sullen sky, lingers sadly, and will not come to an end. It appeared to me to begin two hours ago, and yet it is still light enough to see. Before us, distinguishable as yet to sight or imagination, lie two sections of a forest, unfolding itself beyond range of vision, the contours of its more distant section almost lost in darkness. Colder still grows the wind, and my heart contracts with the still more painful impression of a backward plunge, without shelter and without refuge, into primeval barbarism.

"Every evening at this hour, Colonel, for the last week, we have had our little shower of shells. If you have time to stay a short while you will see how quickly they fire and almost without aiming."

As for time, well, I have really hardly any to spare, and, besides, I have had other opportunities of observing how quickly they fire "almost without aiming." Sometimes it might be mistaken for a display of fireworks, and it is to be supposed that they have more projectiles than they know what to do with. Nevertheless I shall be delighted to stay a few minutes longer and to witness the performance again in their company.

Ah! to be sure, a kind of whirring in the air like the flight of partridges—partridges travelling along very fast on metal wings. This is a change for us from the muffled voice of the cannonade we heard just before; it is now beginning to come in our direction. But it is much too high and much too far to the left—so much too far to the left that they surely cannot be aiming at us; they cannot be quite so stupid. Nevertheless we stop talking and listen with our ears pricked—a dozen shells, and then no more.

"They have finished," the men tell me then; "their hour is over now, and it was for our comrades down there. You have no luck, Colonel; this is the very first time that it was not we who caught it, and, besides, you would think they were tired this evening, the Boches."

It is dark and I ought to be far away. Moreover, they are all going to sleep, for obviously they cannot risk showing a light; cigarettes are the limit of indulgence. I shake hands with a whole line of soldiers and leave them asleep, poor children of France, in their dormitory, which in the silence and darkness has grown as dismal as a long, common grave in a cemetery.

VI

THE PHANTOM BASILICA

October, 1914.

To gaze upon her, our legendary and wonderful basilica of France, to bid her a last farewell before she should crumble away to her inevitable downfall, I had ordered a *détour* of two hours in my service motor car at the end of some special duty from which I was returning.

The October morning was misty and cold. The hillsides of Champagne were deserted that day, and their vineyards with dark brown leaves, wet with rain, seemed to be wrapped completely in a kind of shining fleece. We had also passed through a forest, keeping our eyes open and our weapons ready in case of a meeting with Uhlan marauders.

At last, far away in the fog, uplifting all its great height above a sprinkling of reddish squares, doubtless the roofs of houses, we saw the form of a mighty church. This was evidently the basilica.

At the entrance to Rheims there are defences of all kinds: stone barriers, trenches, *chevaux de frise,* sentinels with crossed bayonets. To gain admission it is not sufficient to be in uniform and military accoutrements; explanations have to be made and the countersign given.

In the great city where I am a stranger, I have to ask my way to the cathedral, for it is no longer in sight. Its lofty grey silhouette, which, viewed from afar, dominated everything so imposingly, as a castle of giants would dominate the houses of dwarfs, now seems to have crouched down to hide itself.

"To get to the cathedral," people reply, "you must first turn to the right over

WAR 55

there, and then to the left, and then to the right, etc."

And my motor car plunges into the crowded streets. There are many soldiers, regiments on the march, motor-ambulances in single file, but there are many ordinary footfarers, too, unconcerned as if nothing were happening, and there are even many well-dressed women, with prayer-books in their hands, in honour of Sunday.

At a street-crossing there is a gathering of people in front of a house whose walls bear signs of recent damage, the reason being that a shell has just fallen there. It is just one of their little brutal jests, so to speak; we understand the situation, look you; it is a simple pastime, just a matter of killing a few persons, on a Sunday morning for choice, because there are more people in the streets on Sunday mornings. But it seems, indeed, as if this town had reconciled itself to its lot, to live its life watched by the remorseless binoculars, under the fire of savages lurking on the neighbouring hillside. The wayfarers stop for a moment to look at the walls and the marks made by the shell-bursts, and then they quietly continue their Sunday walk. This time, we are told, it is women and little girls who lie weltering in their blood, victims of that amiable pleasantry. We hear about it, and then think no more of the matter, as if it were of the smallest importance in times such as these.

This quarter of the town is now deserted. Houses are closed; a silence as of mourning prevails. And at the far end of a street appear the tall grey gates, the lofty pointed arches with their marvellous carvings and the soaring towers. There is no sound; there is not a living soul in the square where the phantom basilica still stands in majesty, where the wind blows cold and the sky is dark.

The basilica of Rheims still keeps its place as if by miracle, but so riddled and rent it is, that it seems ready to collapse at the slightest shock. It gives the impression of a huge mummy, still erect and majestic, but which the least touch would turn into ashes. The ground is strewn with its precious fragments. It has been hastily enclosed with a hoarding of white wood, and within its bounds lies, in little heaps, its consecrated dust, fragments of stucco, shivered panes of glass, heads of angels, clasped hands of saints, male and female. The calcined stone-work of the tower on the left, from top to bottom, has assumed a strange colour like that of baked flesh, and the saints, still standing upright in rank on the cornices, have been decorticated, as it were, by fire. They have no longer either faces or fingers, yet, still retaining their human form, they resemble corpses ranged in rows, their contours but faintly defined under a kind of reddish shroud.

We make a circuit of the square without meeting anyone, and the hoarding which isolates the fragile, still wonderful phantom is everywhere firmly closed.

As for the old palace attached to the basilica, the episcopal palace where the kings of France were wont to repose on the day of their coronation, it is nothing more than a ruin, without windows or roof, blackened all over by tongues of flame.

What a peerless jewel was this church, more beautiful even than *Notre-Dame de Paris,* more open to the light, more ethereal, more soaringly uplifted with its columns like long reeds, astonishingly fragile considering the weight they bear, a miracle of the religious art of France, a masterpiece which the faith of our ancestors had wakened into being in all its mystic purity before the sensual ponderousness of that which we have agreed to call the Renaissance had come to us from Italy, materialising and spoiling all. Oh, how gross, how cowardly, how imbecile was the brutality of those who fired those volleys of scrap-iron with full force against tracery of such delicacy, that had stayed aloft in the air for centuries in confidence, no battles, no invasions, no tempests ever daring to assail its beauty.

That great, closed house yonder in the square must be the archbishop's palace. I venture to ring at the door and request the privilege of entering the church.

"His Eminence," I am told, "is at Mass, but would soon return, if I would wait."

And while I am waiting, the priest, who acts as my host, tells me the history of the burning of the episcopal palace.

"First of all they sprinkled the roofs with I know not what diabolical preparation; then, when they threw their incendiary bombs, the woodwork burnt like straw, and everywhere you saw jets of green flame which burned with a noise like that of fireworks."

Indeed the barbarians had long prepared with studied foresight this deed of sacrilege, in spite of their idiotically absurd pretexts and their shameless denials. That which they had desired to destroy here was the very heart of ancient France, impelled as much by some superstitious fancy as by their own brutal instincts, and upon this task they bent their whole energy, while in the rest of the town nothing else, or almost nothing, suffered damage.

"Could no attempt be made," I ask, "to replace the burnt roof of the basilica, to cover over as soon as possible these arches, which will not otherwise withstand the ravages of next winter?"

"Undoubtedly," he replies, "there is a

risk that at the first falls of snow, the first showers of rain, all this will crumble to ruins, more especially as the calcined stones have lost their power of resistance. But we cannot even attempt to preserve them a little, for the Germans do not let us out of their sight. It is the cathedral, always the cathedral, that they watch through their field-glasses, and as soon as a single person appears in the bell turret of a tower the rain of shells begins again. No, there is nothing to be done. It must be left to the grace of God."

On his return, His Eminence graciously provides me with a guide, who has the keys of the hoarding, and at last I penetrate into the ruins of the basilica, into the nave, which, being stripped bare, appears the loftier and vaster for it.

It is cold there and sad enough for tears. It is perhaps this unexpected chill, a chill far more piercing than that of the world without, which at first grips you and disconcerts you. Instead of the somewhat heavy perfume that generally hangs about old basilicas, smoke of so much incense burned there, emanations of so many biers blessed by the priests, of so many generations who have hastened there to wrestle and pray—instead of this, there is a damp, icy wind which whistles through crevices in the walls, through broken windows and gaps in the vaults. Towards those vaults up yonder, pierced here and there by shrapnel, the eyes are raised, immediately, instinctively, to gaze at them. The sight is led up towards them, as it were, by all those columns that jut out, shooting aloft in sheaves, for their support. They have flying curves, these vaults, of exquisite grace, so designed, it seems, that they may not hinder prayers in their upward flight, nor force back to earth a gaze that aims at heaven. One never grows tired of bending the head backwards to gaze at them, those sacred vaults hastening to destruction. And then high up, too, quite high up, throughout the whole length of the nave, is the long succession of those almost ethereal pointed arches which support the vaults and arches, alike, yet not rigidly uniform, and so harmonious, despite their elaborate carving, that they give rest to the eye that follows them upwards in their soaring perspective. These vast ceilings of stone are so airy in appearance, and moreover so distant, that they do not oppress or confine the spirit. Indeed they seem freed from all heaviness, almost insubstantial.

Moreover, it is wiser to move on under that roof with head turned upward and not to watch too closely where the feet may fall, for that pavement, reverberating rather sadly, has been sullied and blackened by charred human flesh. It is known that on the day of the conflagration the church was full of wounded Germans lying on straw mattresses, which caught fire, and a scene of horror ensued, worthy of a vision of Dante; all these beings, their green wounds scorched by the flames, dragged themselves along screaming, on red stumps, trying to win through doors too narrow. Renowned, too, is the heroism of those stretcher-bearers, priests and nuns, who risked their lives in the midst of falling bombs in their attempt to save these unhappy wretches, whom their own German brothers had not even thought to spare. Yet they did not succeed in saving all; some remained and were burnt to death in the nave, leaving unseemly clots of blood on the sacred flagstones, where formerly processions of kings and queens had slowly trailed their ermine mantles to the sound of great organs and plain-song.

"Look," said my guide, showing me a

wide hole in one of the aisles, "this is the work of a shell which they hurled at us yesterday evening. And now come and see the miracle."

And he leads me into the choir where the statue of Joan of Arc, preserved it may be said by some special Providence, still stands unharmed, with its eyes of gentle ecstasy.

The most irreparable disaster is the ruin of those great glass windows, which the mysterious artists of the thirteenth century had piously wrought in meditation and dreams, assembling together in hundreds, saints, male and female, with translucent draperies and luminous aureoles. There again German scrap-iron has crashed through in great senseless volleys, shattering everything. Irreplaceable masterpieces are scattered on the flagstones in fragments that can never be reassembled —golds, reds and blues, of which the secret has been lost. Vanished are the transparent rainbow colours, perished those saintly personages, in the pretty simplicity of their attitudes, with their small, pale, ecstatic faces; a thousand precious fragments of that glasswork, which in the course of centuries has acquired an iridescence something in the manner of opals, lie on the ground, where indeed they still shine like gems.

To-day there is silence in the basilica, as well as in the deserted square around it; a deathlike silence within these walls, which for so long had vibrated to the voice of organs and the old ritual chants of France. The cold wind alone makes a kind of music this Sunday morning, and at times when it blows harder there is a tinkling like the fall of very light pearls. It is the falling of the little that still remained in place of the beautiful glass windows of the thirteenth century, crumbling away entirely, beyond recovery.

A whole splendid cycle of our history which seemed to live in the sanctuary, with a life almost tangible, though essentially spiritual, has suddenly been plunged into the abyss of things gone by, of which even the memory will soon pass away. The great barbarism has swept through this place, the modern barbarism from beyond the Rhine, a thousand times worse than the barbarism of old times, because it is doltishly, outrageously self-satisfied, and consequently fundamental, incurable, and final—destined, if it be not crushed, to overwhelm the world in a sinister night of eclipse.

In truth it is strange how that statue of Joan of Arc in the choir has remained standing calm, intact, immaculate, without even the smallest scratch upon her gown.

VII

THE FLAG WHICH OUR NAVAL BRIGADE DO NOT YET POSSESS

December, 1914.

At first they were sent to Paris, those dear sailors of ours, so that the duty of policing the city, of maintaining order, enforcing silence and good behaviour might be entrusted to them—and I could not help smiling; it seemed so incongruous, this entirely new part which someone had thought fit to make them play. For truth to tell, between ourselves, correct behaviour in the streets of towns has never been the especial boast of our excellent young friends. Nevertheless by dint of making up their minds to it and assuming an air of seriousness, they had acquitted themselves almost with honour up to the moment when they were freed from that insufferable constraint and were sent outside the city to guard the posts in the entrenched camp. That was already a little better, a little more after their own hearts. At last came a day of rejoicing and glorious intoxication, when they were told that they were all going into the firing-line.

If they had had a flag that day, like their comrades of the land-forces, I will not assert that they would have marched away with more enthusiasm and gaiety, for that would have been impossible, but assuredly they would have marched more proudly, mustered around that sublime bauble, whose place nothing can ever take, whatever may be said or done. Sailors, more perhaps than other men, cherish this devotion to the flag, fostered in them by the touching ceremonial observed on our ships, where to the sound of the bugle the flag is unfurled each morning and furled each evening, while officers and crew bare their heads in silence, in reverent salute.

Yes, they would have been well pleased, our Naval Brigade, to have had a flag wherewith to march into the firing-line, but their officers said to them:

"You will certainly be given one in the end, as soon as you have won it yonder."

And they went away singing, all with the same ardour of heroes; all, I say, not only those who still uphold the admirable traditions of our Navy of old, but even the new recruits, who were already a little corrupted—no more than superficially, however—by disgusting, anti-military claptrap, but who had suddenly recovered their senses and were exalted at the sound of the German guns. All were united, resolute, disciplined, sobered, and dreaming of having a flag on their return.

They were sent in haste to Ghent to cover the retreat of the Belgian Army, but on the way they were stopped at Dixmude, where the barbarians with pink skins like boiled pig were established in ten times their number, and where at all costs a stand was to be made to prevent the abominable onrush from spreading farther.

They had been told:

"The part assigned to you is one of danger and gravity; we have need of your courage. In order to save the whole of our left wing you must sacrifice yourselves until reinforcements arrive. *Try to hold out at least four days.*"

And they held out twenty-six mortal days. They held out almost alone, for reinforcements, owing to unforeseen difficulties, were insufficient and long in coming. And of the six thousand that marched away, there are to-day not more than three thousand survivors.

They had the bare necessities of life and

hardly those. When they left Paris, where the weather was warm and summery, they did not anticipate such bitter cold. Most of them wore nothing over their chests except the regulation jumper of cotton, striped with blue, and light trousers, with nothing underneath, on their legs, and over all that, it is true, infantry greatcoats to which they were unaccustomed and which hampered their movements. For provisions they had nothing but some tins of *confiture de singe*.[1] Naturally no one was prepared for what was practically isolation for twenty-six long days. In the same circumstances ordinary troops, even though their peers in courage, could never have been equal to the occasion. But they had that faculty of fighting through, common to seafaring men, which is acquired in the course of arduous voyages, in the colonies, among the islands, and thanks

---

[1] Military slang term for tins of preserved meat.

to which a true sailor can face any emergency—a special way with them, after all so natural and moreover so merry withal, so tempered with ingratiating tact that it offends nobody.

Well, then, they had fought through; for after those three or four epic weeks, in which day and night they had battled like devils, in fire and water, the survivors were found well-nourished, almost, and with hardly a cold among them.

The only reproach, which I heard addressed to them by their officers, who had the honour to command them in the midst of the furnace, was that they could not reconcile themselves to the practice of crawling. Crawling is a mode of progression introduced into modern warfare by German cunning, and it is well known that our soldiers have to be prepared for it by a long course of training. Now there had not been time to accustom these men to the practice, and when it came to an attack they set out indeed as ordered, dragging themselves along on all fours, but, promptly carried away by their zeal, they stood up to get into their stride, and too many of them were mown down by shrapnel.

One of them told me yesterday, in the words I now quote, how his company having been ordered to transfer themselves to another part of the battle front—but without letting themselves be seen, walking along, bent double, at the bottom of a long interminable trench—were really unable to obey the order literally.

"The trench was already half full of our poor dead comrades. And you will understand, sir, that in places where there were too many of them, it would have hurt us to walk on them; we could not do it. We came out of the ditch, and ran as fast as our legs would carry us along the slope of the parapet, and the Boches who saw us made haste to kill us. But," he continued, "except for trifling acts of disobedience such as that, I assure you, sir, that we behaved very well. Thus I remember some officers commanding sharp-shooters and some officers of light infantry, who had witnessed the Battles of the Marne and the Aisne. Well, when they came sometimes to chat with our officers, we used to hear them say, 'Our soldiers they were brave fellows enough, to be sure! But to see your sailors fighting is an absolute eye-opener all the same.' "

And that town of Dixmude, where they contrived to hold out for twenty-six days, became by degrees something like an anteroom of hell. There were rain, snow, floods, churning up black mud in the bottom of the trenches; blood splashing up everywhere; roofs falling in, crushing wounded in confused heaps or dead bodies in all stages of decomposition; cries and death rattles unceasing, mingling with the continual crash of thunder close at hand. There was fighting in every street, in every house, through broken windows, behind fragments of walls—such close hand-to-hand fighting that sometimes men were locked together trying to strangle one another. And often at night, when already men could no longer tell where to strike home, there were bewildering acts of treachery committed by Germans, who would suddenly begin to shout in French:

"Cease fire, you fools! It is our men who are there and you are firing on your own comrades."

And men lost their heads entirely, as in a nightmare, from which they could neither rouse themselves nor escape.

At last came the day when the town was taken. The Germans suddenly brought up terrific reinforcements of heavy artillery, and heavy shells fell all round like hail—those enormous shells, the devil's own, which make holes six to eight yards wide by four yards deep. They came at the rate of fifty or sixty a minute, and in the craters they made there was at once a jumbled mass of masonry, furniture, carpets, corpses, a chaos of nameless horror. To continue there became truly a task beyond human endurance; it would have meant a massacre to the very last man, moreover without serving any useful purpose, for the abandonment of that mass of ruins, of that charnel-house, which was all that remained of the poor little Flemish town, was no longer a matter of importance. It had resisted just the necessary length of time. The essential point was that the Germans had been prevented from crossing over to the other bank of the Yser, at a time when, nevertheless, all the chances had seemed in their favour; the essential point was this especially, that they would never at any time cross over, now that reinforcements had arrived to hold them up in the south, and now that the floods were encroaching everywhere, barring the way in the north. On this side the barbarians' thrust was definitely countered. And it was our Naval Brigade, who almost by themselves, unwavering in the face of overwhelming numbers, had there supported our left wing, though losing *half* of their effective and eighty per cent. of their officers.

Then they said to themselves, those who were left of them:

"Our flag—we shall get it this time."

Besides, officers in high command, touched and amazed at so much bravery, had promised it to them, and so had the head of the French Government himself, one day when he came to congratulate them.

But alas! they have not yet received it, and perhaps it will never be theirs, unless those officers in high command, to whom I have referred, who have partly pledged their word, intervene while there is yet time, before all these deeds of heroism have fallen into oblivion.

For God's sake give them their flag, our Naval Brigade! And even before sending it to them it would be well, methinks, to decorate it with the Cross.

P. S.—Last week the Naval Brigade were mentioned at the head of the Army Orders of the day, *for having given proof of the greatest energy and complete devotion to duty in the defence of a strategic position of great importance.*

VIII

TAHITI AND THE SAVAGES WITH PINK SKINS LIKE BOILED PIG

November, 1914.

After the lapse of so many years, and in the midst of those moods of rage and anguish or of splendid exaltation which characterise the present hour, I had quite forgotten the existence of a certain enchanted isle, very far away, on the other side of the earth, in the midst of the great Southern Ocean, rearing among the warm clouds of those regions its mountains, carpeted with ferns and flowers. In our October climate, already cold, here in this district of Paris, bare of leaves and in autumn colouring, where I have lived for a month, whence you have but to withdraw a little way to the north in order to

WAR

hear the cannon crashing incessantly like a storm, and where each day countless graves are prepared for the burial of the most precious and cherished sons of France—here the name of Tahiti seems to me the designation of some visionary Eden. I can no longer bring myself to believe that my sojourn in former days in that far-away island was an actual fact. It is with an effort that I recall to my memory that sea, bordered with beaches of pure white coral, the palm trees with arching fronds, and the Maoris living in a perpetual dream, a childlike race with no thought beyond singing and garlanding themselves with flowers.

Tahiti, the island of which I had thought no more, has just been abruptly recalled to my mind by an article in a newspaper, in which it is stated that the Germans have passed that way, pillaging everything. And the commander of the two cruisers, who, without running any risk to themselves, be it understood, committed this dastardly outrage on a poor little open town lying there all unsuspecting, cannot claim to have had any order issued to them from their horrible Emperor—no, indeed, since they were at the other end of the world. All by themselves they had found this thing to do, and of their own accord they did it, from sheer Teutonic savagery.

Yesterday in one of the forts of Paris garrisoned by our sailors, I met an old naval petty officer who, in former days, had on two or three occasions sailed under my orders. He seems to me to have found the name most appropriate to the Prussians and one that deserves to stick to them.

"Well you see, Commander," he said to me, "you and I have often visited together all kinds of savages whom I should have thought the biggest brutes of all, savages with black skins, with yellow skins, or with red skins, but I now see clearly that there is another sort still—those other dirty savages with pink skins like boiled pig, who are much the worst of all."

And so Tahiti the Delectable, where blood had never before been shed, a little Eden, harmless and confiding, set in the midst of mighty oceans—Tahiti has just suffered the visitation of savages with pink skins like boiled pig. So without profit, as without excuse, simply for the sport of the thing, for the pure German pleasure of wreaking as much evil as possible, never mind upon whom, never mind where, these savages, indeed "that worst kind of all," amused themselves by making a heap of ruins in that Bay of Papeete with its eternal calm, under trees ever green, among roses ever in flower.

It is true this happened in the Antipodes, and it is so trifling, so very trifling a matter, compared with the smoking charnel-houses which in Belgium and France were landmarks in the track of the accursed army. But nevertheless it is especially deserving of being brought up again as a still more peculiarly futile and fatuous act of ferocity.

IX

A LITTLE HUSSAR

December, 1914.

His name was Max Barthou. He was one of those dearly loved only sons whose death shatters two or three lives at least, and already we had too nearly forgotten all the skill and courage on his father's part to which we owed the Three Years' Service Bill, without which all France today would be prostrate under the heel of the Monster.

To be sure he, young Max, had done no more than all those thousands of others who have given their lives so gloriously. It is not, then, on that account that I have chosen to speak of him in a special manner. No; one of my chief reasons, no doubt, is that his parents are very dear friends of mine. But it is also for the sake of the boy himself, for whom I had a great affection; moreover, I take a melancholy pleasure in mentioning what a charming little fellow he was. In the first place he had contrived to remain a child, like boys of my own generation long ago, and this is very rare among young Parisians of to-day, most of whom, although this sort of thing is now being brought under control, are at eighteen insufferable little wiseacres. To remain a child! How much that implies, not freshness alone, but modesty, discernment, good sense, and clear judgment! Although he was very learned, almost beyond his years, he had contrived to remain simple, natural, devoted to hearth and home, which he seldom left for more than a few hours in the day, when he went to attend his lectures.

During my flying visits to Paris, when I chanced to be dining with his parents on special days as their only guest, I used to talk to him in spite of the charming shyness he displayed, and each time I appreciated still more deeply his gentle, profound young soul. I can still see him after dinner in the familiar drawing-room, where he would linger with us for a moment before going away to finish his studies. On those occasions, unconventional though it may have been, he would lean against his mother's knee so as to be closer to her, or even lie on the rug at her feet, still playing the part of a coaxing child, teasing the while—oh, very gently, to be sure—an old Siamese cat which had been the companion of his earliest years and now growled at everyone except him. Good God, it was only yesterday! It was only last spring that this little hero, who has just fallen a victim to German shrapnel, would tumble about on the floor, playing with his friend, the old growling cat.

But what a transformation in those three months! It is scarcely a week since I met in a lobby at General Headquarters a smart and resolute blue hussar, who, after having saluted correctly, stood looking at me, not venturing to address me, but surprised that I did not speak to him. Ah! to be sure, it was young Max, whom, at first sight, I had not recognised in his new kit—a young Max of eighteen, greatly changed by the magic wand of war, for he had suddenly grown into a man, and his eyes now shone with a sobered joy. At last he had obtained his heart's desire; to-morrow he was to set out for Alsace for the firing-line.

"So you have got what you wanted, my young friend," I said to him. "Are you pleased?"

"Oh yes, I am pleased."

That, to be sure, was clear from his appearance, and I bade him good-bye with a smile, wishing him the luck to win that splendid medal, that most splendid of all medals, which is fastened with a yellow ribbon bordered with green. I had indeed no foreboding that I had just shaken his hand for the last time.

What insinuating perseverance he had brought to bear in order that he might get to the Front, for his father, though to be sure he would have made no attempt to keep him back, had a horror of doing anything to force on his destiny, and only yielded step by step, glad of heart, yet at the same time in agony at seeing his boy's splendid spirit developing so rapidly.

First of all he had to let him volunteer; then when the boy was chafing with impatience in the *dépôts* where our sons are trained for the firing-line he had to obtain permission for him to leave before his turn. The commander-in-chief, who had welcomed him with pleasure, had wished to keep him by his side, but he protested, gently but firmly, on the occasion of a visit his father paid to the general headquarters.

"I feel too much sheltered here, which is absurd considering the name I bear. Ought I not, on the contrary, to set an example?"

And with a sudden return to that childlike gaiety which he had had the exquisite grace to preserve, hidden under his soldier's uniform, he added with the smile of old days:

"Besides, papa, as the son of the Three Years' Service Bill, it is up to me to do at least three times as much of it as anyone else."

His father, need I say, understood—understood with all his heart—understood so well that, divided between pride and distress, he asked immediately that the boy might be sent to Alsace.

And he had scarcely arrived yonder—
at Thann, on the day of a bombardment—
when a senseless volley of Germany shrapnel, whence it came none knew, without
any military usefulness, and simply for
the pleasure of doing harm, shattered him
like a thing of no account. He had no
time to do "thrice as much as anyone else,"
alas no! In less than a minute that young
life, so precious, so tenderly cherished, was
extinguished for ever.

Four others, companions of his dream
of glory, fell at his side, killed by the same
shell, and the next day they were all committed to the care of that earth of Alsace
which had once more become French.

And in his honour, poor little blue hussar, the people of Thann, who since yesterday were German no longer, desired of
their own accord to make some special
demonstration, because he was the son of
the Three Years' Service Bill. These

Alsatians, released from bondage, had the fancy to adorn his coffin with gilding, simple but charming, as if for a little prince in a fairy-tale, and they carried him in their arms, him alone, while his companions were borne along behind him on a cart.

After the service in the old church the whole assembly, at least three thousand in number, were warned that it would be exceedingly dangerous to go any farther. As the cemetery was in an exposed position, spied upon by German binoculars, the long procession ran a great risk of attracting the barbarians' shrapnel fire, for it was unlikely that they would miss such an excellent opportunity of taking life. But no one was afraid, no one stayed behind, and the little hussar was escorted by them all to the very end.

And there are thousands and thousands of our sons mown down in this manner—

WAR 93

sons from villages or castles, who were all
the hope of, all that made life worth living for, mothers, fathers, grandfathers,
and grandmothers. Night and day for eighteen years, twenty years, they had been
surrounded with every care, brooded over
with all tenderness. Anxious eyes had
watched unremittingly their physical and
moral growth. For some of them, of
humbler families, heavy sacrifices had
necessarily to be made and privations endured so that their health might be assured
and their minds have scope to expand, to
gain knowledge of the world, to be enriched with beautiful impressions. And
then, suddenly, there they are, these dear
boys, prepared for life with such painstaking love; there they are, beloved young
heroes, with shattered breast or brains
blown out—by order of that damnable
Jack-pudding who rules in Berlin.

Oh, execrations and curses upon the

monster of ferocity and trickery who has unchained all this woe! May his life be greatly prolonged so that he may at least have time to suffer greatly; and afterwards may he still live on and remain fully conscious and lucid of intellect in the hour when he shall cross the threshold of eternity, where upon that door, which will never again be opened, may be read, flaming in the darkness, that sentence of utmost horror, *"All hope abandon, ye who enter here."*

X

AN EVENING AT YPRES

"In anticipation of death I make this confession, that I despise the German nation on account of its infinite stupidity, and that I blush to belong to it."

SCHOPENHAUER.

"The character of the Germans presents a terrible blend of ferocity and trickery. They are a people of born liars. One must see this to believe it."

VELLEIUS PATERCULUS,
In the year 10 of the Christian era.

March, 1915.

Ruins in a mournful light which is anxious, seemingly, to fade away into a premature darkness. Vast ruins, ruins of such delicacy! Here is a deployment of those exquisite, slender colonnades and those archways of mysterious charm, which at first sight conjure up for the mind the Middle Ages and Gothic Art in its fair but transient blossoming. But in general, surviving specimens of that Art were only to be found in isolated examples, in the form of some old church or old cloister, surrounded by things of modern growth, whereas at Ypres, there is an *ensemble;* first a cathedral with additions of complicated supplementary buildings, that might be called palaces, whose long façades with their clock-towers present to the eye their succession of windows with pointed arches. As an architectural group it is almost unique in the world, actually a whole quarter of a town, built in little columns, little arches and archaic stone tracery.

The sky is low, gloomy, tormented, as in dreams. The actual night has not yet begun to fall, but the thick clouds of northern winters cast upon the earth this kind of yellowish obscurity. Round about the lofty ruins, the open spaces are full of soldiers standing still, or slowly making their rounds, all with a certain air of seriousness, as if remembering or expecting some event, of which everyone is aware, but which no one discusses. There are also women poorly dressed, with anxious faces, and little children, but the humble population of civilians is merged in a crowd of rough uniforms, almost all of them faded and coated with earth, obviously returned after prolonged engagements. The yellow khaki uniforms of the English and the almost black uniform of the Belgians mingle with the "horizon" blue of greatcoats worn by our French soldiers, who are in a majority; all these different shades blend into an almost neutral colour scheme, and two or three red burnouses of Arab chiefs strike a vivid note, unexpected, disconcerting, in that crowd, coloured like the misty winter evening.

Here are ruins indeed, but on closer inspection, inexplicable ruins, for their collapse seems to date from yesterday, and the crevices and gaps are unnaturally white among the greyish tints of the façades or towers, and here and there, through broken windows, on the interior walls is visible the glittering of gilding. Indeed it is not time that has wrought these ravages—time had spared these wonders—nor yet until our own days, even in the midst of the most terrible upheavals and most ruthless conquest, had men ever attempted to destroy them. No one had dared the deed until the coming of those savages, who are still there, close at hand, crouching in their holes of muddy earth, perfecting each day their idiotic work, and multiplying their volleys of scrap-iron, wreaking their vengeance on these sacred objects whenever they are seized again by an access of rage in consequence of a new repulse.

Near the mutilated cathedral, that palace of a hundred windows, which in the main still stands, is the famous Cloth Hall, built when Flanders was at the height of her glory, a building vulgarised in all its aspects by reproductions, ever since the vindictiveness of the barbarians rendered it still more famous. One November night, it will be remembered, it blazed with sinister magnificence, side by side with the church and the precious buildings surrounding it, illuminating with a red light all the open country. The Germans had brought up in its honour the best that they could muster of incendiary material; their benzine bombs consumed the Hall and then all that it contained; all the treasures that had been preserved there for centuries, its state-rooms, its wainscoting, its pictures, its books, all burned like straw. Now that it is bereft of its lofty roof it has acquired something rather Venetian and surprising in its appearance, with its long façades pierced with uninterrupted rows of floreated pointed arches. In the midst of its irremediable disorder, it is strange and charming. The symmetrical turrets, slender as minarets, set in the angles of the walls, have hitherto escaped those insensate bombs and rise up more boldly than ever, whereas the woodwork of the pointed roofs no longer soars with them up into the air. But the belfry in the centre, which ever since the Middle Ages has kept watch over the plains, is to-day hatefully disfigured, its summit clean cut off, shattered, cleft from top to bottom. It is scarcely in a condition to offer further resistance; a few more shells, and it will collapse in one mass. On one of its sides, very high up, still hangs the monumental dial of a ruined clock, of which the hands point persistently to twenty-five minutes past four—doubtless the tragic moment at which this giant among Flemish belfries received its death blow.

Around the great square of Ypres, where these glories of past ages had so long been preserved for us intact, several houses, the majority of them of ancient Flemish architecture, have been eviscerated in like manner, without object, without excuse, their interior visible from outside through great, gaping holes. But this the barbarians did not do on purpose; it was merely that they happened to be too near, these houses, too closely adjacent to the targets they had chosen, the cathedral and the old palace. It is known that everywhere here, as at Louvain, at Arras, at Soissons, at Rheims, their greatest delight is to direct their fire at public buildings, ruining again and again all that is famous for beauty, art or memories. So then, except for its historic square, the town of Ypres has not suffered very greatly. Ah, but wait! I was forgetting the hospital yonder, which likewise served them for target; for the matter of that the Germans have notoriously a preference for bombarding places of refuge, shelters for wounded and sick, ambulances, first-aid stations and Red Cross wagons.

These acts of destruction, transforming into a rubbish heap that tranquil country of Belgium, which was above everything an incomparable museum, all are agreed to stigmatise as a base, ignoble crime. But it is more than that, it is a masterpiece of the crassest stupidity—the stupidity that Schopenhauer himself could not forbear to publish in the frank outburst evoked by his last moments; for after all it amounts to signing and initialling the ignominy of Germany for the edification of neutrals and of generations to come. The bodies of men tortured and hanged, of women and children shot or mutilated, will soon moulder away completely in their poor, nameless graves, and then the world will remember them no more. But these imperishable ruins, these innumerable ruins of museums or churches, what overwhelming and damning evidence they are, and how everlasting!

After having done all this it is perhaps still more foolish to deny it, to deny it in the very face of such incontrovertible evidence, to deny it with an effrontery that leaves us Frenchmen aghast, or even to invent pretexts at whose childish imbecility we can only shrug our shoulders. "A people of born liars," said the Latin writer. Yes, and a people who will never eradicate their original vices, a people who, moreover, actually dared, despite the most irrefutable written documents, to deny the premeditation of their crimes and the treachery of their attack. What absurd childishness they reveal in their impostures! And who can be the simpletons whom they hope to deceive?

The light is still fading upon the desolate ruins of Ypres, but how slowly to-day! That is because even at noon the light was scarcely stronger on this dull day of March; only at this hour a certain atmosphere, indefinite and sad, broods upon the distant landscape, indicating the approach of night.

They look instinctively at the ruins, these thousands of soldiers, taking their evening walk in such melancholy surroundings, but generally they remain at a distance, leaving the ruins to their magnificent isolation. However, here are three of them, Frenchmen, probably new-comers, who approach the ruins hesitatingly. They advance until they stand under the little arches of the tottering cathedral with a sober air, as if they were visiting tombs. After contemplating them at first in silence, one of them suddenly ejaculates a term of abuse (to whom it is addressed may be easily imagined!), doubtless the most insulting he can find in the French language, a word that I had not expected, which first makes me smile and then, the next moment, impresses me on the contrary as a valuable discovery.

"Oh those hooligans!"

Here the intonation is missing, for I am unable to reproduce it, but in truth the compliment, pronounced as he pronounced it, seems to me something new, worth adding to all the other epithets applied to Germans, which are always pitched in too low a key and moreover too refined; and he continues to repeat, indignant little soldier that he is, stamping with rage:

"Oh those hooligans among hooligans!"

At last the fall of night is upon us, the true night, which will put an end here to all signs of life. The crowd of soldiers gradually melts away along streets already dark, which, for obvious reasons, will not be lighted. In the distance the sound of the bugle summons them to their evening soup in houses or barracks, where they will fall asleep with no sense of security, certain of being awakened at any moment by shells, or by those great monsters that explode with a crash like thunder. Poor, brave children of France, wrapped in their bluish overcoats, none can foresee at what hour death will be hurled at them, from afar, blindly, through the misty darkness —for the most playful fancy presides over this bombardment; now it is an endless rain of fire, now only a single shell which comes and kills at haphazard. And patiently awaiting the rest of the great drama lie the ruins, enveloped in silence. Here and there a little timid light appears in some house still inhabited, where the windows are pasted over with paper to enable them to resist the shock of explosions close at hand, and where the air-holes of the cellars of refuge are protected by sandbags. Who would believe it? Stubborn people, people too old or too poor to flee, have remained at Ypres, and others even are beginning to return, with a kind of fatalistic resignation.

The cathedral and the great belfry project only their silhouettes against the sky, and these seem to have been congealed, gesturing with broken arms. As the night enfolds the world more completely in its thick mists, memory conjures up the mournful surroundings in which Ypres is now lost, deep plains unpeopled and soon plunged in darkness, roads broken up, impassable for fugitives, fields blotted out or mantled with snow, a network of trenches where our soldiers, alas! are suffering cold and discomfort, and so near, hardly a cannon-shot away, those other ditches, more grim, more sordid, where men of ineradicable savagery are watching, always ready to spring out in solid masses, uttering Red Indian war whoops, or to crawl sneakingly along to squirt liquid fire upon our soldiers.

But how the twilight has lengthened in these last few days! Without looking at the clock it is evident that the hour is late, and the mere fact of still being able to see conveys in spite of all a vague presage of April; it seems that the nightmare of winter is coming to an end, that the sun will reappear, the sun of deliverance, that softer breezes, as if nothing unusual were happening in the world, will bring back flowers and songs of birds to all these scenes of desolation, among all these thousands of graves of youth. There is yet another sign of spring, three or four little girls, who rush out into the deserted square in wild spirits, quite little girls, not more than six years old; they have escaped, fleet of foot, from the cellar in which they sleep, and they take hands and try to dance a round, as on an evening in May, to the tune of an old Flemish song. But another child, a big girl of ten, a person in authority, comes along and reduces them to silence, scolding them as if they had done something naughty, and drives them back to the underground dwellings, where, after they have said their prayers, lowly mothers will put them to bed.

Unspeakably sad seemed that childish round, tentatively danced there in solitude at the fall of a cold March night, in a square dominated by a phantom belfry, in a martyred city, in the midst of gloomy, inundated plains, all in darkness, and all beset with ambushes and mourning.

Since this chapter was written the bombardment has continued, and Ypres is now no more than a shapeless mass of calcined stones.

XI
AT THE GENERAL HEADQUARTERS OF THE BELGIAN ARMY

March, 1915.

To-day on my way to the General Headquarters of the Belgian Army, whither I am bound on a mission from the President of the French Republic to His Majesty King Albert, I pass through Furnes, another town wantonly and savagely bombarded, where at this hour of the day there is a raging storm of icy wind, snow, rain, and hail, under a black sky.

Here as at Ypres the barbarians bent their whole soul on the destruction of the historical part, the charming old town hall and its surroundings. It is here that King Albert, driven forth from his palace, established himself at first. Thereupon the Germans, with that delicacy of feeling to which at present no one in the world disputes their claim, immediately made this place their objective, in order to bombard it with their brutal, heavy shells. I need hardly say that there was scarcely anyone in the streets, where I slowed down my motor so that I might have leisure for a better appreciation of the effects of the Kaiser's "work of civilisation"; there were only some groups of soldiers, fully armed, some with their coat-collars turned up, others with the back curtains of their service-caps turned down. They hastened along in the squalls, running like children, and laughing good-humouredly, as if it were very amusing, this downpour, which for once was not of fire.

How is it that there is no atmosphere of sadness about this half-empty town? It is as if the gaiety of these soldiers, in spite of the gloomy weather, had communicated itself to the ruined surroundings. And how full of splendid health and spirits they seem! I see no more on any faces that somewhat startled, haggard expression, common at the beginning of the war. The outdoor life, combined with good food, has bronzed the cheeks of these men whom the shrapnel has spared, but their principal support and stay is their complete confidence, their conviction that they have already gained the upper hand and are marching to victory. The invasion of the Boches will pass away like this horrible weather, which after all is only a last shower of March; it will all come to an end.

At a turning, during a lull in the storm, I come very unexpectedly upon a little knot of French sailors. I cannot refrain from beckoning to them, as one would beckon to children whom one had suddenly found again in some distant jungle, and they come running to the door of my car equally delighted to see someone in naval uniform. They seem to be picked men; they have such gallant, comely faces and such frank, spirited eyes. Other sailors, too, who were passing by at a little distance and whom I had not called, come likewise and surround me as if it were the natural thing to do, but with respectful familiarity, for are we not in a strange country, and at war? Only yesterday, they tell me, they arrived a whole battalion strong, with their officers, and they are camping in a neighbouring village while waiting to "down" the Boches. And I should like so much to make a *détour* and pay them a visit in their own camp if I were not pressed for time, tied down to the hour of my audience with His Majesty. Indeed it gives me pleasure to associate with our soldiers, but it is a still greater delight to associate with our sailors, among whom I passed forty years of my life. Even before I caught sight of them, just from hearing them talk, I could recognise them for what they were. More than once, on our military thoroughfares in the north, on a pitch-dark night, when it was one of their detachments who stopped me to demand the password, I have recognised them simply by the sound of their voices.

One of our generals, army commander on the Northern Front, was speaking to me yesterday of that pleasant, kindly familiarity which prevails from the highest to the lowest grade of the military ladder, and which is a new tone characteristic of this essentially national war in which we all march hand in hand.

"In the trenches," he said to me, "if I stop to talk to a soldier, other soldiers gather round me so that I may talk to them too. And they are becoming more and more admirable for their high spirits and their brotherliness. If only our thousands of dead could be restored to us what a benefit this war would have bestowed upon us, drawing us near together, until we all possess but one heart."

It is a long way to the General Headquarters. Out in the open country the weather is appalling beyond description. The roads are broken up, fields flooded until they resemble marshes, and sometimes there are trenches, *chevaux de frise,* reminding the traveller that the barbarians are still very near. And yet all this, which ought to be depressing, no longer succeeds in being so. Every meeting with soldiers—and the car passes them every minute—is sufficient to restore your serenity. They have all the same cheerful faces, expressive of courage and gaiety. Even the poor sappers, up to their knees in water, working hard to repair the shelter pits and defences, have an expression of gaiety under their dripping service-caps. What numbers of soldiers there are in the smallest villages, Belgian and French, very fraternally intermingling. By what wonderful organisation of the commissariat are these men housed and fed?

But who asserted that there were no Belgian soldiers left? On the contrary, I pass imposing detachments on their way to the front, in good order, admirably equipped, and of fine bearing, with a convoy of excellent artillery of the very latest pattern. Never can enough be said in praise of the heroism of a people who had every reason for not preparing themselves for war, since they were under the protection of solemn treaties that should have preserved them forever from any such necessity, yet who, nevertheless, sustained and checked the brunt of the attack of the great barbarism. Disabled at first and almost annihilated, yet they are recovering themselves and gathering around their sublimely heroic king.

It is raining, raining, and we are numb with cold, but we have arrived at last, and in another moment I shall see him, the King, without reproach and without fear. Were it not for these troops and all these service motor cars, it would be impossible to believe that this remote village was the General Headquarters. I have to leave the car, for the road which leads to the royal residence is nothing more than a footpath. Among the rough motor cars standing there, all stained with mud from the roads, there is one car of superior design, having no armorial bearings of any kind, nothing but two letters traced in chalk on the black door, S.M. (*Sa Majesté*), for this is *his* car. In this charming corner of ancient Flanders, in an old abbey, surrounded by trees and tombs, here is his dwelling. Out in the rain, on the path which borders on the little sacred cemetery, an aide-de-camp comes to meet me, a man with the charm and simplicity that no doubt likewise characterise his sovereign. There are no guards at the entrance to the dwelling, and no ceremony is observed. At the end of an unimposing corridor where I have just time to remove my overcoat, in the embrasure of an opening door, the King appears, erect, tall, slender, with regular features and a surprising air of youth, with frank eyes, gentle and noble in expression, stretching out his hand in kindly welcome.

In the course of my life other kings and emperors have been gracious enough to receive me, but in spite of pomp, in spite of the splendour of some of their palaces, I have never yet felt such reverence for sovereign majesty as here, on the threshold of this little house, where it is infinitely exalted by calamity and self-sacrifice; and when I express this sentiment to King Albert he replies with a smile, "Oh, as for my palace," and he completes his phrase with a negligent wave of the hand, indicating his humble surroundings. It is indeed a simple room that I have just entered, yet by the mere absence of all vulgarity, still possessing distinction. A bookcase crowded with books occupies the whole of one wall; in the background there is an open piano with a music-book on the stand; in the middle a large table, covered with maps and strategic plans; and the window, open in spite of the cold, looks out on to a little old-world garden, like that of a parish priest, almost completely enclosed, stripped of its leaves, melancholy, weeping, as it were, the rains of winter.

After I have executed the simple mission entrusted to me by the President of the Republic, the King graciously detains me a long time in conversation. But if I felt reluctant to write even the beginning of these notes, still more do I hesitate to touch upon this interview, even with the utmost discretion, and then how colourless will it seem, all that I shall venture to say! It is because in truth I know that he never ceases to enjoin upon those around him, "Above all, see that people do not talk about me," because I know and understand so well the horror he professes for anything resembling an "interview." So then at first I made up my mind to be silent, and yet when there is an opportunity of making himself heard, who would not long to help to spread abroad, to the utmost of his small ability, the renown of such a name?

Very striking in the first place is the sincere and exquisite modesty of his heroic nature; it is almost as if he were unaware that he is worthy of admiration. In his opinion he has less deserved the veneration which France has devoted to him, and his popularity among us, than the least of his soldiers, slain for our common defence. When I tell him that I have seen even in the depths of the country, in peasants' cottages, the portraits of the King and Queen of the Belgians in the place of honour, with little flags, black, yellow and red, piously pinned around them, he appears scarcely to believe me; his smile and his silence seem to answer:

"Yet all that I did was so natural. Could a king worthy of the name have acted in any other way?"

Now we talk about the Dardanelles, where in this hour serious issues hang in the balance; he is pleased to question me about ambushes in those parts, which I frequented for so long a time, and which have not ceased to be very dear to me. But suddenly a colder gust blows in through the window, still opening on to the forlorn little garden. With what kindly thoughtfulness, then, he rises, as any ordinary officer might have done, and himself closes the window near which I am seated.

And then we talk of war, of rifles, of artillery. His Majesty is well posted in everything, like a general already broken in to his craft.

Strange destiny for a prince, who, in the beginning, did not seem designated for the throne, and who, perhaps, would have preferred to go on living his former somewhat retired life by the side of his beloved princess. Then, when the unlooked-for crown was placed upon his youthful brow, he might well have believed that he could hope for an era of profound peace, in the midst of the most peaceful of all nations, but, contrary to every expectation, he has known the most appallingly tragic reign of all. Between one day and the next, without a moment's weakness, without even a moment's hesitation, disdainful of compromises, which for a time, at least, though to the detriment of the civilisation of the world, might have preserved for a little space his towns and palaces, he stood erect in the way of the Monster's onrush, a great warrior king in the midst of an army of heroes.

To-day it is clear that he has no longer a doubt of victory, and his own loyalty gives him complete confidence in the loyalty of the Allies, who truly desire to restore life to his country of Belgium; nevertheless, he insists that his soldiers shall co-operate with all their remaining strength in the work of deliverance, and that they shall remain to the end at the post of danger and honour. Let us salute him with the profoundest reverence.

Another less noble, might have said to himself:

"I have amply paid my debt to the common cause; it was my troops who built the first rampart against barbarism. My country, the first to be trampled under the feet of these German brutes, is no more than a heap of ruins. That suffices."

But no, he will have the name of Belgium inscribed upon a yet prouder page, by the side of Serbia, in the golden book of history.

And that is the reason why I met on my way those inestimable troops, alert and fresh, miraculously revived, who were on their way to the front to continue the holy struggle.

Before him let us bow down to the very ground.

Night is falling when the audience comes to an end and I find myself again on the footpath that leads to the abbey. On my return journey, along those roads broken up by rain and by military transport wagons, I remain under the charm of his welcome. And I compare these two monarchs, situated, as it were, at opposite poles of humanity, the one at the pole of light, the other at the pole of darkness; the one yonder, swollen with hypocrisy and arrogance, a monster among monsters, his hands full of blood, his nails full of torn flesh, who still dares to surround himself with insolent pomp; the other here, banished without a murmur to a little house in a village, standing on a last strip of his martyred kingdom, but in whose honour rises from the whole civilised earth a concert of sympathy, enthusiasm, magnificent appreciation, and for whom are stored up crowns of most pure and immortal glory.

XII

SOME WORDS UTTERED BY HER MAJESTY, THE QUEEN OF THE BELGIANS

"All the world knows what value to attach to the King of Prussia and his word. There is no sovereign in Europe who has not suffered from his perfidy. And such a king as this would impose himself upon Germany as dictator and protector! Under a despotism which repudiates every principle, the Prussian monarchy will one day be the source of infinite calamity, not only to Germany, but likewise to the whole of Europe."

THE EMPRESS MARIA THERESA.

March, 1915.

Far away, far away and out of the world seems this place where the persecuted Queen has taken refuge. I do not know how long my motor car, its windows lashed by rain, has rolled along in the dim light caused by showers and approaching night, when at last the Belgian non-commissioned officer, who guided my chauffeur along these unfamiliar roads, announces that we have arrived. Her Majesty, Queen Elizabeth of the Belgians, has deigned to grant me an audience at half-past six, and I trembled lest I should be late, for the way seemed interminable through a countryside which it was too dark to see; but we were in time, punctual to a moment. At half-past six on an evening in March, under an overcast sky, it is already dark as night.

The car stops and I jump out on to the sands of the seashore; I recognise the sound of the ocean close at hand, and the boundless expanse of the North Sea, less dark than the sky, is vaguely perceptible to the sight. Rain and cold winds rage around us. On the dunes two or three houses without lights in the windows are visible as greyish outlines. However, someone carrying a little shining glass lamp is hurrying to receive me; he is an officer in Her Majesty's service, carrying one of those electric torches which the wind does not blow out, and which in France we call an Apache's lantern.

On entering the first house to which the aide-de-camp conducts me, I attempt to leave my overcoat in the hall.

"No, no," he says, "keep it on; we have still to go out of doors to reach Her Majesty's apartments."

This first villa shelters only ladies-in-waiting and officers of that court now so shorn of ceremony, and every evening it is plunged purposely in darkness as a precaution against shrapnel fire. A moment later I am summoned to Her Majesty's presence. Escorted by the same pleasant officer with his lantern, I hurry across to the next house. The rain is mingled with white butterflies, which are flakes of snow. Very indistinctly I see a desert-like landscape of dunes and sands almost white, stretching out into infinity.

"Would you not imagine it a site in the Sahara?" says my guide. "When your Arab cavalry came here the illusion was complete."

It is true, for even in Africa the sands turn pale in the darkness, but this is a Sahara transported under the gloomy sky of a northern night, and it has assumed there too deep a melancholy.

In the villa we enter a warm, well-lighted room, which, with its red furnishings, introduces a note of gaiety, almost of comfort, into this quasi-solitude, battered by wintry squalls. And there is a pleasure, which at first transcends everything else—the physical pleasure of approaching a fireplace with a good blazing fire.

WAR

While waiting for the Queen I notice a long packing-case lying on two chairs; it is made of that fine, unequalled, white carpentry which immediately reminds me of Nagasaki, and on it are painted Japanese letters in columns. The officer's glance followed mine.

"That," he says, "is a magnificent ancient sabre which the Japanese have just sent to our King."

I, personally, had forgotten them, those distant allies of ours in the Farthest East. Yet it is true that they are on our side; how strange a thing! And even over there the woes of these two gracious sovereigns are universally known, and the Japanese desired to show their special sympathy by sending them a valuable present.

I think this charming officer was going to show me the sabre from Japan, but a lady-in-waiting appears, announcing Her Majesty, and he withdraws at once.

"Her Majesty is coming," says the lady-in-waiting.

The Queen, whom I have never yet seen, consecrated as it were by suffering, with what infinite reverence I await her coming, standing there in front of the fire while wind and snow continue to rage in the black night outside. Through which door will she enter? Doubtless by that door over there at the end of the room, on which my attention is involuntarily concentrated.

But no! A soft, rustling sound makes me turn my head towards the opposite side of the room, and from behind a screen of red silk which concealed another door the young Queen appears, so near to me that I have not room to make my court bow. My first impression, necessarily furtive as a flash of lightning, a mere visual impression, I might say a colourist's impression, is a dazzling little vision of blue —the blue of her gown, but more especially the blue of her eyes, which shine like two luminous stars. And then she has such an air of youth; she seems this evening twenty-four, and scarcely that. From the different portraits I had seen of Her Majesty, portraits so little faithful to life, I had gathered that she was very tall, with a profile almost too long, but on the contrary, she is of medium height, and her face is small, with exquisitely refined features—a face almost ethereal, so delicate that it almost vanishes, eclipsed by those marvellous, limpid eyes, like two pure turquoises, transparent to reveal the light within. Even a man unaware of her rank and of everything concerning her, her devotion to duty, the superlative dignity of her actions, her serene resignation, her admirable, simple charity, would say to himself at first sight:

"The woman with those eyes, who may she be? Assuredly one who soars very

high and will never falter, who without
even a tremor of her eyelids can look in
the face not only temptations, but likewise
danger and death.''

With what reverent sympathy, free from
vulgar curiosity, would I fain catch an
echo of that which stirs in the depths of
her heart when she contemplates the drama
of her destiny. But a conversation with
a queen is not directed by one's own fancy,
and at the beginning of the audience Her
Majesty touches upon different subjects
lightly and gracefully as if there were
nothing unusual happening in the world.
We talk of the East, where we have both
travelled; we talk of books she has read;
it seems as if we were oblivious of the
great tragedy which is being enacted,
oblivious of the surrounding country,
strewn with ruins and the dead. Soon,
however, perhaps because a little bond of
confidence has established itself between

us, Her Majesty speaks to me of the destruction of Ypres, Furnes, towns from which I have just come; then the two blue stars gazing at me seem to me to grow a little misty, in spite of an effort to keep them clear.

"But, madam," I say, "there still remains standing enough of the walls to enable all the outlines to be traced again, and almost everything to be practically reconstructed in the better times that are in store."

"Ah," she answers, "rebuild! Certainly it will be possible to rebuild, but it will never be more than an imitation, and for me something essential will always be lacking. I shall miss the soul which has passed away."

Then I see how dearly Her Majesty had already loved those marvels now ruined, and all the past of her adopted country, which survived there in the old stone tracery of Flanders.

Ypres and Furnes incline us to subjects less impersonal, and gradually we at last come to talk of Germany. One of the sentiments predominant, it seems, in her bruised heart is that of amazement, the most painful as well as the most complete amazement, at so many crimes.

"There has been some change in them," she says, in hesitating words. "They used not to be like this. The Crown Prince, whom I knew very well in my childhood, was gentle, and nothing in him led one to expect—— Think of it as I may, day and night, I cannot understand—— No, in the old days they were not like this, of that I am sure."

But I know very well that they were ever thus (as indeed all of us know); they were always the same from the beginning under their inscrutable hypocrisy. But how could I venture to contradict this Queen, born among them, like a beautiful, rare flower among stinging nettles and brambles? To be sure, the unleashing of their latent barbarism which we are now witnessing is the work of that King of Prussia who is the faithful successor of him whom formerly the great Empress Maria Theresa stigmatised; it is he indeed, who, to use the bitter yet very just American expression, has given them swelled heads. But their character was ever the same in all ages, and in order to form a judgment of their souls, steeped in lies, murders, and rapine, it is sufficient to read their writers, their thinkers, whose cynicism leaves us aghast.

After a moment's pause in which nothing is heard but the noise of the wind outside, remembering that the young martyred Queen was a Bavarian princess, I venture to recall the fact that the Bavarians in the Germany Army were troubled at the persecutions endured by the Queen of the Belgians, who had sprung from their own race, and indignant when the Monster who leads this Witches' Sabbath even tried to single out her children as a mark for his shrapnel fire.

But the Queen, raising her little hand from where it rested on the silken texture of her gown, outlines a gesture which signifies something inexorably final, and in a grave, low voice she utters this phrase which falls upon the silence with the solemnity of a sentence whence there is no appeal:

"It is at an end. Between *them* and me has fallen a curtain of iron which will never again be lifted."

At the same time, at the remembrance of her childhood, doubtless, and of those whom she loved over there, the two clear blue eyes which were looking at me grow very misty, and I turn my head away so that I may not seem to have noticed.

XIII

AN APPEAL ON BEHALF OF THE SERIOUSLY WOUNDED IN THE EAST

June, 1915.

The Orient, the Dardanelles, the Sea of Marmora—the mere enunciation of these words, especially in these beautiful months of summer, conjures up images of sun-steeped repose, a repose perhaps a little mournful because of the lack of all movement in those parts, but a repose of such adorable melancholy, in the midst of so many remembrances of great past destinies of humanity, which, throughout these regions, slumber, preserved under the mantle of Islam. But lately on this peninsula of Gallipoli, with its somewhat bare and stony hills, there used to be, in the winding folds of every river, tranquil old villages, with their wooden houses built on the site of ancient ruins, their white minarets, their dark cypress groves, sheltering some of those charming gilded *stelae,* which exist in countless numbers, as everyone knows, in that land of Turkey where the dead are never disturbed. And it was all so calm, all this; it seemed that these humble little Edens might have felt sure of being spared for a long time yet, if not for ever.

But alas! the Germans are the cause of the horror that is unchained here to-day, that horror without precedent, which it is their genius to propagate as soon as they have chosen a spot wherein to stretch out their tentacles, visible or concealed. And it has become a most sinister chaos, lighted by huge flames, red or livid, in a continuous din of hell. Everything is overthrown in confusion and ruin.

"The ancient castles of Europe and Asia are nothing more than ruins," writes to me one of our old Zouaves, who is fighting in those parts; "it is to me unspeakably painful to see those idyllic landscapes harrowed by trenches and shells; the venerable cypress trees are mown down; funereal marbles of great artistic value are shattered into a thousand fragments. If only Stamboul at least may be preserved!"

There are trenches, trenches everywhere. To this form of warfare, underground and treacherous, which the Germans have invented, the Turks, like ourselves, have necessarily had to submit. And so this ancient soil, the repository of the treasures of antiquity, has been ploughed up into deep furrows, in which appear at every moment the fragments of some marvel dating from distant, unknown epochs.

And at every hour of the night and day these trenches are reddened with blood, with the blood of our sons of France, of our English friends, and even of those gentle giants of New Zealand, who have followed them into this furnace. The earth is abundantly drenched with their blood, the blood of all these Allies, so dissimilar, but so firmly united against the monstrous knavery of Germany. Opposite, very close, there flows the blood of those Turks, who are nothing but the unhappy victims of hateful plots, yet who are so freely insulted in France by people who understand nothing of the underlying cause. They fall in thousands, these Turks, more exposed to shrapnel fire than our own men; nevertheless they fight reluctantly; they fight because they have been deceived and because insolent foreigners drive them on with their revolvers. If on the whole they fight none the less superbly, it is merely a question of race. And the simplest of them, who have been persuaded that they had to do with only their Russian enemies, are unaware that it is we who are there.

On this peninsula we occupy a position won and retained by force of heroism. The formation of the ground continues to render our situation one of difficulty and our tenacity still more worthy of admiration. Our position, indeed, is dominated by the low hills of Asia, where the forts have not yet all been silenced; there is therefore no nook or corner, no tent, no single one of our field hospitals, where doctors can attend to the wounded in perfect security, absolutely certain that no shell will come and interrupt them.

This terrible void France desires to fill with all possible dispatch. With the utmost haste, she is fitting out a great hospital ship, which the Red Cross Society has offered to provide at its own expense with three hundred beds, with linen, nurses, drugs and dressings. This life-saving ship will be moored in front of an island close to the scene of battle, but completely sheltered; steam and motor launches will be attached to it to fetch those who are seriously wounded and bring them on board day by day, so that they may be operated upon and tended in peace before infection and gangrene set in. How many precious lives of our soldiers will thus be saved!

It must be understood that the stretcher-bearers of the ship will bring back likewise wounded Turks, if there are any lying in the zone accessible to them; and this is only fair give and take, for they do the same for us. Some Zouaves who are fighting there wrote to me yesterday:

"The Turks are resisting with unequalled bravery; this all the newspapers of Europe admit. But our wounded and our prisoners receive excellent treatment from them, as General Gouraud himself announced in an Order of the Day; they nurse them, feed them, and tend them better than their own soldiers."

And here is a literal extract from a letter from one of our adjutants: "I fell, wounded in the leg, beside a Turkish officer more seriously wounded than myself; he had with him emergency dressings and he began by dressing my wound before thinking of his own. He spoke French very well and he said to me, 'You see, my friend, to what a pass these miserable Germans have brought us!'"

If I dwell upon the subject of the Turks it is not, I need hardly say, because I take a deeper interest in them than in our own men; no one will insult me by such a reflection. No. But as for our own soldiers, does not everyone love them already? Whereas these poor fellows are really too much misjudged and slandered by the ignorant masses.

"Spare them as soon as they hold up their hands," said a heroic general, brought home yesterday from the Dardanelles covered with wounds. He was addressing his men in a proclamation admirable for the loyalty of its tone. "Spare them," he said; "it is not they who are our enemies."

So, then, the great life-saving ship which is about to be sent to those parts is being made ready to sail in all haste. But the Red Cross Society have herewith taken upon themselves a heavy responsibility, and it will be readily understood that they will need money, much money. That is why I make this appeal on their behalf to all the world. So much has already been given that it is an earnest wish that still more will be forthcoming, for with us charity is inexhaustible when once the noble impulse stirs. I would ask that help may be given very soon, for there is need of dispatch.

WAR

How greatly this will change the condition of life for our dear soldiers. What confidence it will give them to know that if they fall, seriously wounded, there is waiting for them a place of refuge, like a little corner of France, which is equivalent to saying a corner of Paradise, and that they will be taken there at once. Instead of the miserable makeshift field hospital, too hot and by no means too safe, where the terrible noise never ceases to rack aching temples, there will be this refuge, absolutely out of range of gun fire, this great peaceful ship, open everywhere to the good, wholesome air of the sea, where at last prevails that silence so passionately desired by sufferers, where they will be tended with all the latest improvements and the most ingenious inventions by gentle French nurses in white dresses, whose noiseless footfall disturbs no slumber nor dream.

XIV

SERBIA IN THE BALKAN WAR

July, 1915.

But lately I had included Serbia—its prince in particular—in my first accusations against the Balkan races, when they hurled themselves together upon Turkey, already at grips with Italy. But later on, in the course of so many wrathful indictments, I did not once again mention the name of the Serbians. That was because my information from those parts proved to me clearly that among the original Allies, the Allies of the Balkans, the Serbians were the most humane. They themselves, doubtless, observed that I made no further reference to them, for no insulting letter reached me from their country, whereas Bulgarians and even Greeks poured upon me a flood of unseemly abuse.

Since then the great philanthropist, Carnegie, in order to establish the truth definitely in history, has set on foot a conscientious international court of inquiry, whose findings, published in a large volume, have all the authority of the most impartial official documents. Here are recorded, supported by proofs and signatures, the most appalling testimonies against Bulgarians and Greeks; but noticeably fewer crimes are ascribed to Serbia's account. But this volume entitled "Conquest in the Balkans" (Carnegie Endowment) has, I fear, been too little read, and it is a duty to bring it to the notice of all.

Moreover, who would refuse pardon to that gallant Serbian nation for the excesses they may have committed? Who would not accord to them the profound sympathy of France to-day, when the Prussian Emperor, in his ruthless ferocity, has sacrificed them as a bait for one of his most abominable and knavish plots? Poor little Serbia! With what magnificent heroism she has succeeded in defending herself against an enemy who did not even shrink from the atrocious act of burning her capital at a time when it was peopled solely by women and children! Poor little Serbia, suddenly become a martyr, and sublime! I would willingly at least win back for her some French hearts which my last book may perhaps have alienated. And that is the sole purpose of this letter.

XV

ABOVE ALL LET US NEVER FORGET!

August 1st, 1915.

A year ago to-day began that shameful violation of Belgian territory. In the midst of these appalling horrors, time, it seems, has hastened still more in its bewildered flight, and already we have reached the anniversary of that foul deed, the blackest that has ever defiled the history of the human race. This crime was committed after long, hypocritical premeditation, and no pang of remorse, no vestige of shame, caused those myriads of accomplices to stay their hands. It is a crime that leaves with us, in addition to immeasurable mourning, an impression of infinite sadness and discouragement, because it proves that one of the greatest countries in Europe is hopelessly bankrupt of all that men have agreed to call honour, civilisation, and progress. The barbarian onslaughts of ancient days were not only a thousand times less murderous, but, let it be specially noted, incomparably less revolting in character. There were certain dastardly deeds, certain acts of profanation, certain lies, at which those hordes that came to us from Asia hesitated; an instinctive reverence still restrained them; and, moreover, in those times they did not destroy with such impudent cynicism, invoking the God of Christians in a burlesque pathos of prayer!

Thus in our own day has arisen a grisly Emperor, with a pack of princelings, his own progeny, a litter of wolves, whose most savage and at the same time most cowardly representative wears a death's head upon his helmet; and generals and millions of

Germans have been found ready to unite, after a calculated preparation of nearly half a century, in committing this same preliminary crime, the forerunner of so many others, and by way of prelude, to crush ignobly in their advance a little nation whom they had deemed without defence.

But lo! the little nation arose, quivering with sacred indignation, and attempted to check the great barbarism, suddenly unmasked; to check it for at least a few days, even at the cost of a seemingly inevitable doom of annihilation.

What starry crowns can history award worthy of that Belgian nation and of their King, who did not fear to bid them set themselves there as a barrier.

King Albert of Belgium, dispossessed to-day of his all and banished to a hamlet —what tribute of admiration and homage can we offer him worthy of his acceptance and sufficiently enduring? Upon tablets of flawless marble let us carve his name in deep letters so that it may be well insured against the fugitiveness of our French memories, which, alas! have sometimes proved a little untrustworthy, at least in face of the age-long infamies of Germany. May we remember for ever, we, and even our far distant posterity, that to save civilised Europe, and especially our own country of France, King Albert did not for one moment shrink from those sheer, unconditional sacrifices which seemed beyond human strength. Spurning the tempting compromises offered by that monstrous emperor, he has fulfilled to the end his duty of loyal hero with a calm smile, as if nothing were more natural. And so perfect is his modesty that he is surprised if he is told that he has been sublime.

As for Queen Elizabeth, let each one of

us dedicate to her a shrine in his soul. One of the most dreaded duties that falls almost invariably to the lot of queens is having to reign over adopted countries while exiled from their own. In the special case of this young martyred queen, this doom of exile which has befallen her, and many other queens, must be a far more exquisite torture, added to all the other evils endured, for a crushing fatality has come and separated her for ever from all who were once her own people, even from that noble woman, all devotion and charity, who was her mother. This additional sorrow she bears with calm and lofty courage which never falters. She is by the King's side, his constant companion in the most terrible hours of all; a companion whose energy halts at nothing. And she is by the side of the poor who have lost their all by pillage or fire; by the side of the wounded who are suffering or dying;

to them, too, she is a companion, comforting the lowliest with her adorable simplicity, shedding on all the increasing bounty of her exquisite compassion. Oh, may she be blest, reverenced, and glorified! And for her altar, dedicated within our souls, let us choose very rare, very delicate flowers, like unto herself.

XVI

THE INN OF THE GOOD SAMARITAN

August, 1915.

In spite of the kindly welcome which the visitor receives and a wholesome spirit of gaiety which never fails, it is an inn that I cannot honestly recommend without reserve.

In the first place it is somewhat difficult of access, so much so that ladies are never admitted. To climb up to it—for it is perched very high—the traveller must needs make his way for hours through ancient forests which the axe had spared until a very few months ago, along unknown paths winding at steep gradients; among giant trees, pines or larches, felled yesterday, which still lie about in all directions; paths that are concealed by close-growing greenery with such jealous care that in the few open spaces occurring here and there trees have been planted right into the ground, trees uprooted elsewhere, and which are here only to hide the wayfarer behind their dying branches. It may be supposed that on the neighbouring hills sharp eyes, unfriendly eyes, are watching, which necessitate all these precautions.

But there are many people on the road through those forests, which seemed at first sight virgin. Viewing from a little distance all these mountains covered with the same strong growth of forest, so luxuriant, and everywhere so alike in appearance, who would imagine that they sheltered whole tribes? And such strange tribes, evidently survivors of an entirely prehistoric race of men, and in the anomalous position of having no women-folk. Here are nothing but men, and men all dressed alike, with a singular fancy for uniformity, in old, faded, woollen greatcoats of horizon blue. They have not paid much attention to their hair or beards, and they have almost the appearance of brigands, except that they all have such pleasant faces and such kindly smiles for the wayfarer that they inspire no terror. So far from this he is tempted rather to stop and shake hands with them. But what curious little dwellings they have built, some isolated, some grouped together into a village! Some of them are quite lightly constructed of planks of wood and are covered over with branches of pine, and within are mattresses of leaves that serve for beds. Some are underground, grim as caves of troglodytes, and the approach to them is protected by huge masses of rock, doubtless their defence against formidable wild beasts haunting the neighbourhood. And these dwellings are always close to one of the innumerable streams of clear water which rush down babbling from the heights, among pink flowers and mosses—for these miniature waterfalls are many, and all these mountains are full of the pleasant music of running water. From time to time, to be sure, other sounds are heard, hollow sounds of evil import, detonations on the right or the left, which the echoes prolong. Can it be that there is artillery concealed almost everywhere throughout the forest? What want of taste, thus to disturb the symphony of the springs.

They have probably just arrived here, these savage tribes, dressed in greyish blue; they are recent settlers, for all their arrangements are new and improvised, and so likewise is the interminable winding road which they have laid out, and which to-day our motor cars, with the help of a little goodwill, manage to climb so rapidly.

One of the peculiarities of these hidden villages which crouch in the shade of the lofty forest trees is that each has its own cemetery, tenderly cared for, so close that it almost borders on the dwellings, as if the living were anxious not to sever their comradeship with the dead. But how comes it that death is so frequent among these limpid streams, in a region where the air is so invigorating and so pure? These tombs, so disquieting in their disproportionate numbers, are ranged in rows, all with the same humble crosses of wood. They have borders of ferns carefully watered, or of little pebbles, well selected. Flowers such as thrive in shady places and are common in these parts, shoot up their pretty pink spikes all around, and the whole scene is steeped in the green translucent twilight which envelops the whole mountain, the twilight of these unchanging trees, pines and larches, stretching away into infinity, crowded together like wheat in a field, tall and straight like gigantic masts.

In our haste to reach that Inn of the Good Samaritan, which is our destination, we keep on climbing at a rapid pace, notwithstanding acute-angled corners where our cars have to back before they can effect the turn, and other awkward places where our cars slip on the wet soil, skid, and come to a stop.

These tribes, so primitive in appearance, through whose midst we have been travelling since the morning, seem to be concentrating their energies especially on making these roads, which, one would think, cannot really be necessary to their simple mode of existence. In our onward course we meet nearly all these men, working with might and main, with axes, shovels, stakes and picks, hurrying as if the task were urgent. They stand erect for a moment to salute us, smiling a little with touching and respectful familiarity, and then they bend down again to their arduous work, levelling, enlarging, timbering, or digging out roots that are in the way, and rocks that encroach. And when we were told that it is scarcely ten months since they began this exhausting work in the midst of forest, virgin hitherto, we are fain to believe that all the Genii of the mountains have roused themselves and lent their magic help.

Oh! what tribute of admiration mingled with emotion do we owe to these men, likewise, the builders of roads, our gallant territorials, who seem to be playing at wild men of the woods. They have revived for us the miracles of the Roman Legions who so speedily opened up roads for their armies through the forests of Gaul. Thanks to their prodigious labour, performed without a break, without a murmur, the conditions of warfare in this region, only yesterday still inaccessible, will be radically changed for the benefit of our dear soldiers. Everything will reach them on the heights ten times more expeditiously than before—arms, avenging shells, rations; and in a few hours the seriously wounded will be gently driven down in carriages to comfortable field hospitals in the plains.

Roughly speaking at an altitude of about fourteen or fifteen hundred metres, the ancient forest with its arching trees ends abruptly. The sky is deep blue above our heads, and infinite horizons unfold around us their great spectacular display of illusive images. The air is very clear and pure to-day in honour of our arrival, and it is so marvellously transparent that we miss no detail of the most distant landscapes.

We are told that we have reached the

plateau where stands that hospitable inn; it is, however, not yet in sight. But the plateau itself, where is it situated, in which country of the world? In the foreground around us and below nothing is visible except summits uniformly wooded with trees of the same species; this brings back to mind those great, monstrous expanses of forest which must have covered the entire earth in the beginning of our geological period, but it is characteristic of no particular country or epoch of history. In the distance, it is true, there are signs of a more tell-tale nature. Thus yonder, on the horizon, that succession of mountains, all mantled with the same dark verdure, bears a close resemblance to the Black Forest; that chain of glaciers over there, silhouetting so clearly against the horizon its ridges of rosy crystal, might well be taken for the Alps; and that peak in particular is too strikingly like the

Jungfrau to admit of any doubt. But I may not be more definite in my description; I will merely say that those bluish plains in the East, rolling away at our feet like a great sea, were but lately French, and are now about to become French once more.

How spacious is this plateau, and how naked it stands among all those other summits mantled with trees. Here there is not even brushwood, for doubtless the winter winds rage too fiercely; here nothing grows but short, thick grass and little stunted plants with insignificant flowers. It is ecstasy to breathe here in this delicious intoxication of pure air and of spaciousness and light. And yet there is some vague sense of tragedy about the place, due perhaps to those great round holes, freshly made; to those cruel clefts with which here and there the earth is rent. What can have fallen here from the sky,

WAR

leaving such scars on the level surface? We are warned, moreover, that monstrous birds of a very dangerous kind, with iron muscles, often come and hover about overhead in that fair blue sky. And from time to time a cannon shot from some invisible battery comes to disturb the impressive silence and reverberates in the valleys below; and then comes, long drawn out, the whirring of a shell, like a flight of partridges going past.

We notice some French soldiers, Alpine *chasseurs,* or cavalry on their horses, scattered in groups about this plain, as it may be called, situated at such an altitude. At this moment all lift their heads and look in the same direction; this is because one of those great dangerous birds has just been signalled; it is flying proudly, remote in the open sky, in the clear blue. But immediately it is pursued by white clouds, quite miniature clouds, which give the effect of being created instantaneously, only to vanish as quickly—little explosions of white cotton wool, one might say—and it seems impossible that they should be freighted with death. However, that evil bird has understood; he is aware that good marksmen are aiming at him, and he turns back on hasty wing, while our soldiers gaily burst out laughing.

And the inn? It lies just in front of us, a few hundred paces away; it is that greyish hut with its gay tricolour floating on the light breeze of these altitudes, but near it stands a very lofty cross of pine-wood, four or five yards high, stretching out its arms as in solemn warning.

The fact is, I must admit, that people die very frequently at this Inn of the Good Samaritan or in its neighbourhood, and it is for this reason that in the beginning I recommended it with reserve. It is surprising, is it not, in such health-giving air?

But the truth of it is indisputable, and it has been necessary hurriedly to attach to it a cemetery whose existence this tall cross of pine proclaims from afar to travellers.

Yes, many men die here, but they die so nobly, a death of all deaths most desirable—each according to his own temperament, according to the nature of his soul: some in the calm serenity of duty done, others in magnificent exaltation, but all in glory.

Can this be the famous inn—in other words the dwelling of those officers who command this outpost, and where their friends on rare and brief visits, liaison officers, bearers of dispatches, etc., are sure of finding such cordial and genial hospitality—this modest hutting built of planks? So it is, and that there may be no mistake, there is an imposing signboard in the fashion of old times. Shaped like a shield, it hangs from an iron rod and bears the inscription, "Inn of the Good Samaritan." The legend is painted in ornamental letters, and the humour of it is irresistible among such Crusoe-like destitution. Doubtless one day some officer in a specially happy mood thought of this jest as a welcome for comrades coming thither on special duty. Naturally he found at once among his men one who was a carpenter and another a decorator in civil life, both very much amused at being ordered to put this unpremeditated idea forthwith into execution.

The furniture of the inn is very rough and ready, if the truth be told, and the wall of planks just shelters you from the snow or rain, but from the wind hardly, and from shells not at all. But one fills one's lungs to the full with the air that reaches one through the little windows, and from the threshold, looking downwards, there is a marvellous bird's-eye view of great forests, of an unending chain of glaciers, clear as crystal, of unbounded distances, and even over the tops of clouds.

Ah well! all along the battle front there are such Inns of the Good Samaritan. These others are perched less high, and they do not bear the same name; indeed very often they have no name at all; but in all of them prevails the same spirit of kindly hospitality, firm confidence, smiling endurance and cheerful sacrifice. Here, as there, between two showers of shells, men are capable of amusing themselves with childish trifles, so stout of heart are they, and if access were not forbidden on military grounds I would invite all pessimists in the background, who have doubts of France and of her destiny, to come here for a cure.

And now, having seen the inn, let us pay a pious visit to the annex, the inevitable annex, alas! Around the wooden cross which dominates it is a piece of ground enclosed with an open fence, made of boughs of larch artistically intertwined. Within its bounds those tombs, too numerous already, preserve something of a military aspect, ranged as they are in such correct alignment and all with the same little crosses, adorned with a wreath of greenery. The Cross! In spite of all infidelity, denial, scorn, the Cross still remains the sign to which a tender instinct of atavism recalls us at the approach of death. There is not a tree, not a shrub, for none grow here: on the ground there is only the short grass that grows upon this wind-swept plateau. An attempt has been made, to be sure, to make borders of certain stunted plants found in the neighbourhood, but rows of pebbles last best. And in five weeks or so, thick shrouds of snow will begin to cover up everything, until another spring succeeds the snows and the grass grows green again, in the midst of still deeper oblivion.

Nevertheless let us not pity them, for they have had the better part, these young dead who rest there on that glorious mountain-top which is destined to become once more, after the war, a solitude ineffably calm, high above forest, valley and plain.

XVII
FOR THE RESCUE OF OUR WOUNDED

August, 1915.

The preservation of the lives of our dear wounded, who day by day are stricken down upon the field of battle, depends nine times out of ten on the rapidity with which they are carried in; on the gentleness and promptness with which they are taken to the field hospitals, where they may be put into comfortable beds and left in the care of all the kind hands that are waiting for them. This fact is not sufficiently well known; often it happens that wounds which would have been trifling have become septic and mortal because they have been left too long covered with inadequate, uncleanly bandages, or have trailed for many hours on the earth or in the mud.

In the first weeks of the war when we were taken unawares by the barbarians'

WAR 175

attack, treacherous and sudden as a thunderbolt, it was not bullets and shrapnel alone that killed the sons of France. Often, too, it happened that help was slow in arriving; sufficient haste could not be made, and it was impossible to cope right at the beginning with these shortcomings, in spite of much admirable devotion and ingenuity in multiplying and improving the means of service. Since then helpers have poured in from all sides; gifts have been showered with open hands; organisation has been created with loving zeal, and things are already working very well. But much still remains to be done, for the work is immense and complex, and it is our duty to hold ourselves more than ever in readiness, in anticipation of great final struggles for deliverance.

Now a society is being formed for sending to the Front some fresh squadrons of fast motor-ambulances, furnished with cots and mattresses of improved design.

Thus thousands more of our wounded will be laid immediately between clean sheets, then brought into hospital with all speed, without that delay which is a cause of gangrened wounds, without those jolts that aggravate the pain of fractured bones and inflict yet more grievous suffering on those dear bruised heads.

But in spite of the first magnificent donations, a remainder of the money has still to be found to complete the enterprise satisfactorily. And so I beseech all mothers, whose sons may fall at any moment; I beseech all those who have in the firing-line a kinsman dear to them; I beseech them to send their offerings without hesitation, without calculation, so that soon, before the April battles begin, several hundreds of those great life-saving ambulances may be ready to start, which will assuredly preserve for us a vast number of precious lives.

XVIII
AT RHEIMS

August, 1915.

On a beautiful August evening I am hastening in a motor car towards Rheims, one of our martyred towns, where I am hoping to find shelter for the night before continuing my journey to the General Headquarters of another Army. In order to avoid military formalities I wish to enter the town before the sun sets, and it is already too low for my liking.

The evening is typical of one of our splendid French summers; the air is exquisitely clear, of a delightful, wholesome warmth, tempered with a light, refreshing breeze. On the hillsides of Champagne the beautiful vines on which the grapes are ripening spread a uniform expanse of green carpet, and there are so many trees, so many flowers everywhere, gardens in all the villages, and roses climbing up all the walls.

To-day the cannon is heard no more, and one would be tempted to forget that the barbarians are there close at hand if there were not so many improvised cemeteries all along the road. Everywhere there are these little graves of soldiers, all alike, which are now to be found from end to end of our beloved France, all along the battle front; their simple crosses of wood are ranged in straight lines as if for a parade, topped, some of them, with a wreath; others still more pathetically with a simple service-cap, red or blue, falling to rags. We salute them as we pass.

Among these glorious dead there are some whose kindred will seek them out and bring them back to the province of their birth later, when the barbarians have gone away, while others, less favoured, will remain there forever until the great final day of oblivion. But what masses of flowers people have already been at pains to plant there for them all. Around their resting-place there is a brave show of all shades of brilliant colour, dahlias, cannas, China asters, roses. Who has undertaken this labour of love? Girls from the nearest villages? Or perhaps even their own brothers-in-arms, who dwell on the outskirts everywhere like invisible subterranean tribes in these casemates, trench shelters, dug-outs of every shape covered over with green branches?

This region, you must know, is not very safe, and when we arrive at a section of the road which is too much exposed, a sentinel, especially posted there to give warning, instructs us to leave the high road for a moment, where we should run the risk of being seen and shelled, and to take some sheltered traverse behind the curtains of poplars.

One of my soldier-chauffeurs suddenly turns round to say to me:

"Oh look, sir, there is an Arab cemetery. They have put on each grave their little crescents instead of the cross."

Here to be sure the humble *stelae* of white wood are all topped with the crescent of Islam, and this is something of a shock to us in the very heart of France. Poor fellows, who died for our righteous cause, so far from their mosques and their marabouts they sleep, and alas! without facing Mecca, because they who laid them piously to rest did not know that this was to them a requisite of peaceful slumber! But the same profusion of flowers has been brought to them as to our own countrymen, and I need not say that we salute them likewise—a little late, perhaps, for we pass them so rapidly.

We reach Rheims just before sunset, and here a sudden sadness chills us. All is silent and the streets almost deserted. The shops are closed, and some of the houses seem to gape at us with enormous holes in their walls.

One of the infrequent wayfarers tells us that at the Hotel Golden Lion, Cathedral Square, we may still be able to find someone to take us in, and soon we are at the very foot of the noble ruin, which is still enthroned as majestically as ever in the midst of the martyred town, dominating everything with its two towers of open stone-work. I stop my car, the sound of whose rolling in such a place seems profanation; the sadness of ruins is intensified here into veritable anguish, and the silence is such that instinctively we begin to talk softly, as if we had already entered the great church that has perished.

The Golden Lion—but its panes of glass are broken, the doors stand open, the courtyard is deserted. I send one of my soldiers there, bidding him call, but not too loudly, in the midst of all this mournful meditation. He returns; he has received no reply and has seen holes in the walls. The house is deserted. We must seek elsewhere.

It is twilight. A golden after-glow still lingers around the magnificent summits of the towers, while the base is wrapped in shadow. Oh, the cathedral, the marvellous cathedral! what a work of destruction the barbarians have continued to accomplish here since my pilgrimage of last November. It had ever been a lace-work of stone, and now it is nothing but a lace-work torn in tatters, pierced with a thousand holes. By what miracle does it still hold together? It seems as if to-day the least shock, a breath of wind perhaps, would suffice to cause it to crumble away, to resolve itself, as it were, into scattered atoms. How can it ever be repaired? What scaffolding could one dare to let lean against those unstable ruins. In an attempt to afford it yet a little protection sandbags have been piled up, mountain high, against the pillars of the porticoes, the same precaution that has been taken in the case of St. Mark's in Venice, of Milan, of all those inimitable masterpieces of past ages which are menaced by the refined culture of Germany. Here the precautions are vain; it is too late, the cathedral is lost, and our hearts are wrung with sorrow and indignation as we look this evening upon this sacred relic of our past, our art, and our faith, in its death throes and its abandonment. Ah, what savages! And to feel that they are still there, close at hand, capable of giving it at any hour its *coup de grâce*.

To bid it farewell, perhaps a last farewell, we will walk around it slowly with solemn tread, in the midst of this deathlike silence which seems to grow more intense as the light fails.

But suddenly, just as we are passing the ruins of the episcopal palace, we hear a prelude of sound, a tremendous, hollow uproar, something like the rumbling of a terrible thunderstorm, near at hand and unceasing. And yet the evening sky is so clear! Ah yes, we were warned, we know whence it comes; it is the bombardment of our heavy artillery, which was expected half an hour after sunset, directed at the barbarians' trenches. This is a change for us from the silence, this cataclysmal music, and it contributes to our walk a different kind of sadness, another form of horror. And we continue to gaze at the wonderful stone carving overhanging us—the bold little arches, the immense pointed arches, so frail and so exquisite. Indeed how does it all still hold together? Up above there are little columns which have lost their base and remain, as it were, suspended in the air by their capitals. The windows are no more; the lovely rose-windows have been destroyed; the nave has huge fissures from top to bottom. In the twilight the whole cathedral assumes more and more its phantom-like aspect, and that noise which causes everything to vibrate is still increasing. It is a question whether so many vibrations will not bring about the final downfall of those too fragile carvings which hitherto have held on so persistently at such great heights above our heads.

Here comes the first wayfarer in that solitude, a well-dressed person. He is hurrying, actually running.

"Do not stay there," he shouts to us; "do you not see that they are going to bombard?"

"But it is we, the French, who are firing. It is our own artillery. Come, do not run so fast."

"I know very well that it is we, but each time the enemy revenge themselves on the cathedral. I tell you that there will be a rain of shells here immediately. Look out for yourselves."

He goes on. So much the better; it was kind of him to warn us, but his jacket and his billy-cock jarred upon the melancholy grandeur of the scene.

Where a street opens into the square two girls now appear; they stop and hesitate. Evidently they are aware, these two, that the barbarians have a habit of taking a noble revenge upon the cathedral, and that shells are about to fall. But doubtless they have to cross this square in order to reach their home, to get down into their cellar. Will they have time?

They are graceful and pretty, fair, bareheaded, with their hair arranged in simple bands. They gaze into the air with their eyes raised well up towards the

WAR 187

heavens, perhaps to see if death is beginning to pass that way, but more likely to send up thither a prayer. I know not what last brightness of the twilight, in spite of the encroaching gloom, illumines so delightfully their two upturned faces, and they look like saints in stained-glass windows. Both make the sign of the cross, and then they make up their minds, and hand in hand they run across the square. With their religious gestures, their faces expressing anxiety, yet courage too and defiance, they suddenly seem to me charming symbols of the girlhood of France; they run away, indeed, but it is clear that they would remain without fear if there were some wounded man to carry away, some duty to perform. And their flight seems very airy in the midst of this tremendous uproar like the end of the world.

We are going away too, for it is wiser. In the streets there are a very few wayfarers who are running to take shelter, running with their backs hunched up, although nothing is falling yet, like people without umbrellas surprised by a shower. One of them, who nevertheless does not mind stopping, points out to us the last hotel still remaining open, a "perfectly safe" hotel, he says, over there in a quarter of the town where no shell has ever fallen.

God forbid that I should dream of laughing at them, or fail to admire as much as it deserves their persistent and calm heroism in remaining here, in defiance of everything, in their beloved town, which is suffering more and more mutilations. But who would not be amused at that instinct which causes the majority of mankind to hunch their backs against hail of whatever description? And then, is it because the air is fresh and soft and it is good to be alive that after the unspeakable heartache at the sight of the cathedral and

WAR 189

the passion verging on tears, a calm of reaction sets in and in that moment everything amuses me?

At the end of a quiet street, where the noise of the cannonade is muffled in the distance, we find the hotel which was recommended to us.

"Rooms," says the host, very pleasantly, standing on his doorstep, "oh, as many as you like, the whole hotel if you wish, for you will understand that in times such as these travellers—— And yet as far as shells go you have nothing to fear here."

An appalling din interrupts his sentence. All the windows in the front of the house are shivered to fragments, together with tiles, plaster, branches of trees. In his haste to run away and hide he misses the step on the threshold and falls down flat on his face. A dog who was coming along jumps upon him, full of importance, recalling him to order with a fierce bark. A cat, sprung from I know not where, flies through space like an aerolith, uses my shoulder for a jumping-off place, and is swallowed up by the mouth of a cellar. But words are too tedious for that series of catastrophes, which lasts scarcely as long as two lightning flashes. And they continue to bombard us with admirable regularity, as if timing themselves with a metronome; the wall of the house is already riddled with scars.

It is very wrong, I admit, to take these things as a jest, and indeed with me that impression is only superficial, physical, I might say; that which endures in the depth of my soul is indignation, anguish, pity. But at this entry which the Germans made into our hotel, that peaceful spot, with flourish of their great orchestra, in the presence of so many surprises, how retain one's dignity? There is a fair number of little shells, it seems, but no heavy shells;

they travel with their long whistling sound, and burst with a harsh din.

"Into the cellar, gentlemen," cries the innkeeper, who has picked himself up unhurt. Apparently there is nothing else to be done. I should have come to that conclusion myself. So I turn round to order in my three soldiers too, who had remained outside to look at a hole made by shrapnel in the body of the car. But upon my word I believe they are laughing, the heartless wretches; and then I can restrain myself no longer, I burst out laughing too.

Yes, it is very wrong of us, for presently there will be bloodshed and death. But how resist the humour of it all: the good man fallen flat on his face, the self-importance of the dog, who thought he must put a stop to the situation, and especially the cat, the cat swallowed up by an air-hole after showing us as a supreme exhibition of flight its little hindquarters with its tail in the air.

XIX
THE DEATH-BEARING GAS

November, 1915.

It is a place of horror, conceived, it might be thought, by Dante. The air is heavy, stifling; two or three nightlights, which seem to be afraid of shining too brightly, scarcely pierce the vaporous, overheated darkness which exhales an odour of sweat and fever. Busy people are whispering there anxiously, but the principal sound that is heard is an agonised gasping for breath. This gasping comes from a number of cots, in rows, touching one another, on which are lying human forms, their chests heaving with rapid and laboured breathing, lifting the bedclothes as though the moment of the death-rattle had come.

This is one of our advance field hospitals, improvised, as best might be, the day after one of the most damnable abominations committed by the Germans. The nature of their affliction made it impossible to transfer all these sons of France, from whom seems to come the noise of the death-rattle without hope of recovery, to a place farther away. This large hall with dilapidated walls was yesterday a wine cellar for storing barrels of champagne; these cots—about fifty in number—were made in feverish haste of branches which still retain their bark, and they resemble the kind of furniture in our gardens that we call rustic. But why is there this heat, in which it is almost impossible to draw a natural breath, pouring out from those stoves? The reason for it is that it is never hot enough for the lungs of persons who have been asphyxiated. And this darkness: wherefore this darkness, which gives a Dantesque aspect to this place of torment, and which must be such a hindrance to the gentle, white-gowned nurses? It is because the barbarians are there in their burrows, quite near this village, with the shattering of whose houses and church spire they have more than once amused themselves; and if, at the gloomy fall of a November night, through their ever watchful field-glasses, they saw a range of lighted windows indicating a long hall, they would at once guess that there was a field hospital, and shells would be showered down upon the humble cots. It is well known, this preference of theirs for shelling hospitals, Red Cross convoys, churches.

And so there is scarcely light enough to see through that misty vapour which rises from water boiling in pans. Every minute nurses fetch huge black balloons, and the patients nearest to suffocation stretch out their poor hands for them; they contain oxygen, which eases the lungs and alleviates the suffering. Many of them have these black balloons resting on chests panting for breath, and in their mouths they are holding eagerly the tube through which the life-saving gas escapes. They are like big children with feeding bottles; it adds a kind of grisly burlesque to these scenes of horror. Asphyxia has different effects upon different constitutions, and calls for variety in treatment. Some of the sufferers, lying almost naked on their beds, are covered with cupping-glasses, or painted all over with tincture of iodine. Others even—these alas! are very seriously affected indeed—others are all swollen, chest, arms, and face, and resemble toy figures of blown-up gold-beater's skin. Toy figures of gold-beater's skin, children with feeding bottles—although these comparisons alone are true, yet indeed it seems almost sacrilege to make use of them when the heart is wrung with anguish and you are ready to weep tears of pity and of wrath. But may these comparisons, brutal as they are, engrave themselves all the more deeply upon the minds of men by reason of their very unseemliness, to foster there for a still longer time indignant hatred and a thirst for holy reprisals.

For there is one man who spent a long time preparing all this for us, and this man still goes on living; he lives, and since remorse is doubtless foreign to his vulturine soul, he does not even suffer, unless it be rage at having missed his mark, at least for the present. Before thus unloosing death upon the world he had coldly combined all his plans, had foreseen everything.

"But nevertheless supposing," he said to himself, "my great rhinoceros-like onrushes and my vast apparatus of carnage were by some impossible chance to hurl itself in vain against a resistance too magnificent? In that case I should dare perhaps, calculating on the weakness of neutral nations, I should dare perhaps to defy all the laws of civilisation, and to use other means. At all hazards let us be prepared."

And, to be sure, the onrush failed, and, timidly at first, fearing universal indignation, he tried asphyxiation after exerting himself, be it understood, to mislead public opinion, accusing, with his customary mendacity, France of having been the originator. His cynical hope was justified; there has been, alas! no general arousing of the human conscience. No more at this than at earlier crimes—organised pillage, destruction of cathedrals, outrage, massacres of children and women—have the neutral nations stirred; it seems indeed as if the crafty, ferocious, deathly look of his Gorgon-like or Medusa-like head had frozen them all to the spot. And at the present hour in which I am writing the last to be turned to stone by the Medusa glare of the monster is that unfortunate King of Greece, inconsistent and bungling, who is trembling on the brink of a precipice of most terrible crimes. That some nations remain neutral from fear, that indeed is comprehensive enough; but that nations, otherwise held in the highest repute, can remain pro-German in sentiment, passes our understanding. By what arts have they been blinded, these nations; by what slanders, or by what bribe?

Our dear soldiers with their seared lungs, gasping on their "rustic" cots, seem grateful when, following in the major's footsteps, someone approaches them, and they look at the visitor with gentle eyes when he takes their hand. Here is a man all swollen, doubtless unrecognisable by those who had only seen him before this terrible turgidity, and if you touch his poor, distended cheeks however lightly, the fingers feel the crackling of the gases that have infiltrated between skin and flesh.

"Come, he is better than he was this morning," says the major, and in a low voice meant for the nurse's ear, he continues, "This man too, nurse, I am beginning to think that we shall save. But you must not leave him alone for one moment on any account."

Oh, what unnecessary advice, for she has not the smallest intention of leaving him alone, this white-gowned nurse, whose eyes have already black rings around them, the result of a watch of forty-eight hours without a break. Not one of them will be left alone, oh no! To be sure of this, it is sufficient to glance at all those young doctors and all those nurses, somewhat exhausted, it is true, but so attentive and brave, who will never let them out of their sight.

And, thank heaven, nearly all of them will be saved.[1] As soon as they are well enough to be moved they will be taken far away from this Gehenna at the Front, where the Kaiser's shells delight to hurl themselves upon the dying. They will be put more comfortably to bed in quiet field hospitals, where indeed they will suffer greatly for a week, a fortnight, a month, but whence they will emerge without excessive delay, better advised, more prudent, in haste to return once more to the battle.

It may be said that the scheme of gas attacks has failed, like that other scheme of attacks in great savage onrushes. The result was not what the Gorgon's head had expected, and yet with what accurate calculation the time for these attacks has been selected, always at the most favourable

---

[1] Of six hundred who were gassed that night, more than five hundred are out of danger.

moment. It is well known that the Germans, past masters of the art of spying, and always informed of everything, never hesitate to choose for their attacks of whatever kind, days of relief, hours when newcomers in the trenches opposite to them are still in the disorder of their arrival. So on the evening on which the last crime was committed six hundred of our men had just taken up their advanced position after a long and tiring march. Suddenly in the midst of a volley of shells which surprised them in their first sleep, they could distinguish, here and there, little cautious sibilant sounds, as if made stealthily by sirens. This was the death-bearing gas which was diffusing itself around them, spreading out its thick, gloomy, grey clouds. At the same time their signal lights suddenly ceased to throw out through that mist more than a little dim illumination. Then distracted, already suffocating, they remembered too late those masks which had been given them, and in which in any case they had no faith. They were awkward in putting them on; some of them, feeling the scorching of their bronchia, urged by an irresistible impulse of self-preservation, even yielded to a desire to run, and it was these who were most terribly affected, for, breathing deeply in the effort of running, they inhaled vast quantities of chlorine gas. But another time they will not let themselves be caught in this way, neither these nor any others of our soldiers. Wearing masks hermetically closed, they will station themselves immovably around piles of wood, prepared beforehand, whence sudden flames will arise, neutralising the poisons in the air, and the upshot of it all will be hardly more than an uncomfortable hour, unpleasant while it lasts, but almost always without fatal result. It is true that in those accursed dens which are their laboratories, Germany's learned men, convinced now that the neutral nations will acquiesce in anything, are making every effort to discover worse poisons still for us, but until they have found them, as on so many other occasions, the Gorgon gaze will have missed its mark. So much is certain. We, alas! have as yet found no means of returning them a sufficiently cruel equivalent; we have no defence other than the protective mask, which, however, is being perfected day by day. And, after all, in the eyes of neutral nations, if they still have eyes to see, it is perhaps more dignified to make use of nothing else. At the same time, how very different our position would be if we succeeded in asphyxiating them too, these plunderers, assassins, aggressors, who broke into our country like burglars, and who, despairing of ever bursting through our lines, attempt to smoke us out ignominiously in our own home, in our own dear country of France, as they might smoke out rabbits in their burrows, rats in their holes. No language of man had ever anticipated such transcendent acts of infamy which would revolt the most degraded cannibals, and so there are no names for such acts. Our poor victims of their gas, panting for breath in their cots, how ardently I wish that I could exhibit them to all the world, to their fathers, sons, and brothers, to excite in them a paroxysm of sacred indignation and thirst for vengeance. Yes, exhibit them everywhere, to let everyone hear the death-rattle, even those neutral nations who are so impassive; to convict of obtuseness or of crime all those obstinate Pacificists, and to sound throughout the world the alarm against the barbarians who are in eruption all over Europe.

XX

ALL-SOULS' DAY WITH THE ARMIES AT THE FRONT

2nd November, 1915.

Two or three days ago all along the front of the battle began the great festival in honour of our soldiers' graves. No matter where they lie, grouped around churches in the ordinary village cemeteries, ranged in rows with military precision in little special cemeteries consecrated to them, or even situated singly at the side of a road, in a corner of a wood, or alone and lost in the midst of fields, everywhere, seen from afar off, under the gloomy sky of these November days and against the greyish background of the countryside, they attract the eyes with the brilliant newness of their decorations. Each grave is decked with at least four fine tricolours, their flagstaffs planted in the ground, two at the head, two at the foot, and an infinite number of flowers and wreaths tied with ribbons. It was the officers and the comrades of our dead soldiers who subscribed together to give them all this, and who, sometimes in spite of great difficulties, sent to the neighbouring towns for the decorations, and then arranged them all with such pious care, even on the graves of those of whom little was known, and of those poor men, few in number, whose very names have perished.

Here in this village where I chance to be staying in the course of my journey, the cemetery is built in terraces, and forms an amphitheatre on the side of a hill, and the corner dedicated to the soldiers is high up, visible to all the neighbourhood. There are fifteen of these graves, each with its four flags, making sixty flags in all. And in the bitter autumn wind they flutter almost gaily, unceasingly, all these strips of bunting, they wanton in the air, intermingle, and their bright colours shine out more conspicuously. For the matter of that, no three other colours in combination set off one another so gaily as our three dear colours of France.

And these tombs, moreover, have such quantities and quantities of flowers, dahlias, chrysanthemums and roses, that they seem to be covered with one and the same richly decorated carpet. During these days of festival, the rest of the cemetery is also very full of flowers, but it looks dull and colourless compared with that corner sacred to our soldiers. It is this favoured corner which is visible at first sight, from a distance, from all the roads leading to the village, and wayfarers would ask themselves:

"What festival can they be celebrating with all those flags fluttering in the air?"

Two days before, I remember coming to see the preparations for these ingenious decorations. *Chasseurs,* with their hands full of bunches of flowers, were working there rapidly and thoughtfully, speaking in low tones. In the distance could be heard, though much muffled, the orchestra of the incessant battle in which the magnificent, great voice of our heavy artillery predominated; it seemed like the muttering of a storm all along the distant horizon. It was very gloomy in that cemetery, under an overcast sky, whence fell a semi-darkness already wintry in aspect. But the zeal of these *chasseurs,* who were decking the tombs so well, must yet have solaced the souls of the youthful dead with a little tender gaiety.

And what beautiful, moving Masses were sung for them all along the front on the day of their festival. All the little churches—those at least that the barbarians have not destroyed—had been decorated that day with all that the villages could muster in the way of flags, banners, tapers and wreaths. And they were too small, these churches, to hold the crowds that flocked to them. There were officers, soldiers, civil population, women mostly in mourning, whose eyes under their veils were reddened with secret tears. Some of the soldiers, of their own accord, desiring to honour the souls of their comrades with a very special concert, had taken pains to learn the Judgment hymns, the *Dies iræ,* the *De profundis,* and their voices, unskilfully led though they were, vibrated impressively in the unison of plain-song, which the organ accompanied. Indeed what could better prepare them for the supreme sacrifice and for a death nobly met than these prayers, this music and even these flowers?

They sang this morning, these improvised choristers, with a solemn transport. Then after Mass, in spite of the icy rain and the muddy roads, the crowds that issued from each church in procession betook themselves to the cemeteries, in attendance on the priests bearing the solemn crucifix. And again, as on the day of the funerals, all the little graves were blessed.

If I record these scenes, it is for the sake of mothers and wives and families, living far from here in other provinces of France, whose hearts no doubt grow heavier at the thought that the grave of someone dear to them may be neglected and very soon become unrecognisable. Oh let them take comfort! In spite of the simplicity of these little wooden crosses, almost all alike, nowhere are they cared for and honoured so well as at the front; in no other place could they receive such touching homage, such tribute of flowers, of prayers, of tears.

XXI

THE CROSS OF HONOUR FOR THE FLAG OF THE NAVAL BRIGADE!

Paris, which is above all other towns famous for its noble impulses, was fêting some days ago our Naval Brigade from the Yser—or rather the last survivors of the heroic Brigade, the few who had been able to return. It was well done thus to make much of them, but alas! how soon it will all be forgotten.

To-day, in honour of the Brigade, of which three-quarters were annihilated, our well-beloved and eminent Minister of Marine, Admiral Lacaze, has given instructions that the glorious Order of the Day, in which the commander-in-chief bade them farewell, should be posted up on all our ships of war. It ends with these words:

"The valiant conduct of the Naval Brigade on the plains of the Yser, at Nieuport, and at Dixmude will always be to the Forces an example of warlike zeal and devotion to their country. The Naval Brigade and their officers may well be proud of this new and glorious page which they have inscribed on their records."

Indeed this Order posted up on board the ships will be more permanent than the welcome that Paris gave them; but alas! this likewise will be forgotten, too soon forgotten.

As it was decided when this Brigade of picked men were disbanded to preserve their flag for the Army so that their memory might be perpetuated, could not the Cross of Honour be attached to a flag of such distinction? This idea, it seems, has been entertained, but perhaps—I know nothing of the matter—there is some impeding clause in the regulations, for I seem to remember to have read there that before it can be decorated with the Cross a flag must have been unfurled on the occasion of a great offensive or a splendid feat of arms. Now the case of our Naval Brigade is so unprecedented that no regulations could have made provision for it. How could they have unfurled their flag in that unparalleled conflict since in those days they still had none? This Brigade, hastily organised on the spur of the moment, was thrown into the firing-line without that incomparable symbol, the tricolour, which all the other brigades possessed before they set out. It was not until later, long after the great exploits with which they won their spurs, that their flag was presented to them, at a time when they had a somewhat less terrible part to play. In such circumstances I venture to hope that the regulation may be relaxed in their favour. If this flag of theirs were decorated, all the sailors who received it with such joy over there, that day when all its three colours were still new and brilliant, would feel themselves distinguished at the same time as the flag itself, and later, in future days, when their descendants came to look at it, poor, sacred, tattered remnant, tarnished and dusty, this Cross, which had been awarded, would speak to them more eloquently of sublime deeds done on the Belgian Front.

They can never be too highly honoured, the Naval Brigade, of whom it has been officially recorded:

"No troops in any age have ever done what these have done."

And here is an extract from a letter which, on the day when they were disbanded, after reviewing them for the last time, General Hély d'Oissel wrote to the captain of the *Paillet,* who was then commanding the Brigade, a letter which was read to all the sailors, drawn up in line, and which brought tears to their honest eyes:

"I should be happy to preserve the Brigade State (the terrible roll of dead, officers, non-commissioned officers, and men) as an eloquent witness of the immense services rendered to the country by this admirable Brigade, which the land forces are proud to have had in their ranks, and which I, personally, am proud to have had under my command during more than a year of the war.

"This morning when I saw your magnificent sailors filing past with such cheerfulness and precision, I could not but feel a poignant emotion when I reflected that it was for the last time."

Indeed it was just there, in the blood-drenched marshes of the Yser, that for the second time, and finally, the onrush of the barbarians was broken. The two great decisive reverses suffered by that wretched Emperor of the blood-stained hands were, everyone knows, the retreat from the

Marne and then that check in Belgium, in the face of a very small handful of sailors of superhuman tenacity.

They were not specially selected, these men sublimely stubborn; no, they were the first to hand, chosen hastily from among the men in our ports. They had not even gone away to fight, but quietly to police the streets of Paris, and from Paris, one fine day, in the extremity of our peril, they were dispatched to the Yser, without preparation, inadequately equipped, with barely sufficient food, and told simply:

"Let yourselves be killed, but do not suffer the German beast to pass! At all costs resist for at least a week, to give us time to come to the rescue."

Now they held out, it will be remembered, indefinitely, in the midst of a veritable inferno of fire, shrapnel, clamour, crumbling ruins, cold, rain, engulfing mud, and ever since that day when they brought to a standstill the onrush of the beast,

France felt that she was saved indeed.

Indeed, as a general rule, it is sufficient to take any honest fellows whatsoever, and merely by putting a blue collar on them, you transform them into heroes. In the Chinese expedition, among other instances, I have seen at close quarters the very same thing: a small handful of men, taken haphazard from one of our ships, commanded by very young officers who had only just attained their first band of gold braid, and this assembly of men, hastily mustered, suddenly became a force complete in itself, admirable, united, disciplined, zealous, fearless, capable of performing within a couple of days prodigies of endurance and daring.

Oh that Brigade of the Yser, whose destiny I just missed sharing! I had plotted desperately, I admit, for the sake of being attached to it, and I was about to gain my end when an obstacle arose which I could never have foreseen and which excluded me inexorably. To have to renounce this dream when it was almost within my grasp will be for me unto my life's end a subject of burning and tormenting regret. But at least let me comfort myself a little by paying my tribute of admiration to those who were there. Let me at least have this little pleasure of working to glorify their memory. Therefore I herewith beg on their behalf —not only in my own name, for several of my comrades in the Navy associate themselves in my prayer, comrades who were likewise not among them, the disinterested nature of whose motives cannot consequently be questioned—I beg herewith on their behalf almost confidently, although the regulation may prove me in the wrong, that it may be accorded to them, the distinction they have earned ten times over, at which no one can take umbrage, and that a scrap of red ribbon be fastened to their flag.

XXII
THE ABSENT-MINDED PILGRIM
December, 1915.

That day, during a lull in the fighting, the General gave me permission to take a motor car for three or four hours to go and look for the grave of one of my nephews, who was struck down by a shell during our offensive in September.

From imperfect information I gathered that he must be lying in a humble emergency cemetery, improvised the day after a battle, some five or six hundred yards away from the little town of T—— whose ruins, still bombarded daily and becoming more and more shapeless, lie on the extreme border of the French zone, quite close to the German trenches. But I did not know how he had been buried, whether in a common grave, or beneath a little cross inscribed with his name, which would make it possible to return later and remove the body.

"To get to T——," the General had said, "make a *détour* by the village of B——, that is the way by which you will run the least risk of being shelled. At B——, if the circumstances of the day seemed dangerous, a sentinel would stop you as usual; then you would hide your motor behind a wall, and you could continue your journey on foot—with the usual precautions, you will understand."

Osman, my faithful servant, who has shared my adventures in many lands for twenty years, and who, like everyone else, is a soldier, a territorial, had a cousin killed in the same fight as my nephew, and he is buried, so he was told, in the same cemetery. So he has obtained permission to accompany me on my pious quest.

To-day all that gloomy countryside is

WAR 221

powdered with hoar-frost and over it hangs an icy mist; nothing can be distinguished sixty yards ahead, and the trees which border the roads fade away, enveloped in great white shrouds.

After driving for half an hour we are right in the thick of that inferno of the battle front, which, from habit, we no longer notice, though it was at first so impressive and will later on be so strange to remember. All is chaos, hurly-burly; all is overthrown, shattered; walls are calcined, houses eviscerated, villages in ruins on the ground; but life, intense and magnificent, informs both roads and ruins. There are no longer any civilians, no women or children; nothing but soldiers, horses, and motor cars; of these, however, there are such numbers that progress is difficult. Two streams of traffic, almost uninterrupted, divide the roads between them; on one side is everything that is on its way to the firing-line; on the other side everything that is on its way back. Great lorries bringing up artillery, munitions, rations, and Red Cross supplies jolt along on the frozen cart ruts with a great din of clanging iron, rivalling the noise, more or less distant, of the incessant cannonade. And the faces of all these different men, who are driving along on these enormous rolling machines, express health and resolution. There are our own soldiers, now wearing those bluish helmets of steel, which recall the ancient casque and bring us back to the old times; there are yellow-bearded Russians, Indians, and Bedouins with swarthy complexions. All these crowds are continuously travelling to and fro along the road, dragging all sorts of curious things heaped up in piles. There are also thousands of horses, picking their way among the huge wheels of innumerable vehicles. Indeed it might be thought that this was a general migration of mankind after some cataclysm had subverted the surface of the earth. Not so! This is simply the work of the great Accursed, who has unloosed German barbarism. He took forty years to prepare the monstrous *coup,* which, according to his reckoning, was to establish the apotheosis of his insane pride, but which will result in nothing but his downfall, in a sea of blood, in the midst of the detestation of the world.

There is certainly a remarkable lull here to-day, for even when the rolling of the iron lorries ceases for a moment, the rumbling of the cannon does not make itself heard. The cause of this must be the fog and in other respects, too, how greatly it is to our advantage, this kindly mist; it seems as if we had ordered it.

Here we are at the village of B——, which, the General had expected, would be the terminus of our journey by car.

Here the throng is chiefly concentrated among shattered walls and burnt roofs; helmets and overcoats of "horizon" blue are crowding and bustling about. And every place is blocked with these heavy wagons, which, as soon as they arrive, come to a halt, or take up a convenient position for starting on the return journey. For here we have reached the border of that region where, as a rule, men can only venture by night, on foot, with muffled tread; or if by day, one by one, so that they may not be observed by German fieldglasses. At the end of the village, then, signs of life cease abruptly, as if cut off clean with the stroke of an axe. Suddenly there are no more people. The road, it is true, leads to that town of T——, which is our destination; but all at once it is quite empty and silent. Bordered by its two rows of skeleton trees, white with frost, it plunges into the dense white fog with an air of mystery, and it would not be surprising to read here, on some signpost, "Road to Death."

We hesitate for a moment. I do not, however, see any of the signals which are customary at places where a halt must be made, nor the usual little red flag, nor the warning sentry, holding his rifle above his head with both hands. So the road is considered practicable to-day, and when I ask if indeed it leads to T——, some sergeants who are there salute and confine their answer to the word "Yes, sir," without showing any surprise. So all that we have to do is to continue, taking, nevertheless, the precaution of not driving too fast, so as not to make too much noise.

And it is merely by this stillness into which we are now plunging, by this solitude alone, that I am aware that we are right in the very front; for it is one of the strange characteristics of modern warfare that the tragic zone bordering on the burrows of the barbarians, is like a desert. Not a soul is visible; everything here is hidden, buried, and—except on days when Death begins to roar with loud and terrible voice—most frequently there is nothing to be heard.

We go on and on in a scenery of dismal monotony, continually repeating itself, all misty and unsubstantial in appearance as if made of muslin. Fifty yards behind us it is effaced and shut away; fifty yards ahead of us it opens out, keeping its distance from us, but without varying its aspect. The whitish plain with its frozen cart ruts remains ever the same; it is blurred and does not reveal its distances; there is ever the same dense atmosphere, resembling cold white cotton wool, which has taken the place of air, and ever the two rows of trees powdered with rime, looking like big brooms which have been rolled in salt and thrust into the ground by their handles. It is clear indeed that this region is too often ravaged by lightning, or something equivalent. Oh, how many trees there are shattered, twisted, with splintered branches hanging in shreds!

We cross French trenches running to the right and left of the road, facing the unknown regions towards which we are hastening; they are ready, several lines of them, to meet the improbable contingency of a retreat of our troops; but they are empty and are merely a continuation of the same desert. I call a halt from time to time to look around and listen with ears pricked. There is no sound; everything is as still as if Nature herself had died of all this cold. The fog is growing thicker still, and there are no field-glasses capable of penetrating it. At the very most they might hear us arrive, the enemy, over there and beyond. According to my maps we have still another two miles at least before us. Onwards!

But suddenly there appears to have been an evocation of ghosts; heads, rows of heads, wearing blue helmets, rise together from the ground, right and left, near and far. Upon my soul! they are our own soldiers to be sure, and they content themselves with looking at us, scarcely showing themselves. But for these trenches, which we are passing so rapidly, to be so full of soldiers on the alert, we must be remarkably close to the Ogre's den. Nevertheless let us go a little farther, as the kindly mist stays with us like an accomplice.

Five hundred yards farther on I remember the enemy's microphones, which alone could betray us; and it so happens that the frozen earth and the mist are two wonderful conductors of sound. Then it suddenly occurs to me that I have gone much too far, that I am surrounded by death, that it is only the fog which shelters us, and the thought that I am responsible for the lives of my soldiers makes me shudder. It is because I am not on duty; my expedition to-day is of my own choosing, and in these conditions, if anything happened to one of them, I should suffer remorse for the rest of my life. It is high time to leave the car here! Then I shall continue my journey on foot towards the town of T——, to find out from our soldiers who are installed there in cellars of ruined houses, whereabouts the cemetery lies which I am seeking.

But at this same moment a densely crowded cemetery is visible in a field to the left of the road; there are crosses, crosses of white wood, ranged close together in rows, as numerous as vines in the vineyards of Champagne. It is a humble cemetery for soldiers, quite new, yet already extensive, powdered with rime too, like the surrounding plains, and infinitely desolate of aspect in that colourless countryside, which has not even a green blade of grass. Can this be the cemetery we are seeking?

"Yes, certainly this is it," exclaims Osman, "this is it, for here is my poor cousin's grave. Look, sir, the first, close to the ditch which borders the cemetery. I read his name here."

Indeed, I read it myself, "Pierre D——." The inscription is in very large letters, and the cross is facing in our direction more than the others, as if it would call to us:

"Halt! we are here. Do not run the risk of going any farther. Stop!"

And we stop, listening attentively in the silence. There is no sound, no movement anywhere, except the fall of a bead

of frost, slipping off the gaunt trees by
the wayside. We seem to be in absolute
security. Let us then calmly enter the
field where this humble cross seems to have
beckoned to us.

Osman had carefully prepared two little
sealed bottles, containing the names of our
two dead friends, which he intended to
bury at their feet, fearing lest shells should
still be capable of destroying all the labels
on the graves. It is true we have carelessly
forgotten to bring a spade to dig up the
earth, but it cannot be helped, we shall
do it as best we may. The two chauffeurs
accompany us, for knowing the reason for
our expedition, they had, with kindly
thoughtfulness, each brought a camera to
take a photograph of the graves. Pierre
D—— had been discovered at once. There
remained only my nephew to be found
among these many frozen graves of youthful dead. In order to gain time—for the

place is not very reassuring, it must be confessed—let us divide the pious task among us, and each of us follow one of these rows, ranged with such military regularity.

I do not think human imagination could ever conceive anything so dismal as this huge military cemetery in the midst of all this desolation, this silence which one knows to be listening, hostile and treacherous, in this horrible neighbourhood whose menace seems, as it were, to loom over us. Everything is white or whitish, beginning with the soil of Champagne, which would always be pale even if it were not powdered with innumerable little crystals of ice. There is no shrub, no greenery, not even grass; nothing but the pale, cinder-grey earth in which our soldiers have been buried. Here they lie, these two or three hundreds of little hillocks, so narrow that it seems that space is precious, each one

marked with its poor little white cross.
Garlanded with frost, the arms of all these
crosses seem fringed with sad, silent tears
which have frozen there, unable to fall,
and the fog envelops the whole scene so
jealously that the end of the cemetery cannot be clearly seen. The last crosses, hung
with white drops, are lost in livid indefiniteness. It seems as if this field alone
were left in the world, with all its myriad
pearls gleaming sadly, and naught else.

I have bent down over a hundred graves
at least and I find nothing but unknown
names, often even that cruel phrase, "Not
identified." I say that I have bent down,
because sometimes, instead of being
painted in black letters, the inscription was
engraved on a little zinc plate—nothing
better was to be had—engraved hastily and
difficult to decipher. At last I discover
the poor boy whom I was seeking, "Sergent Georges de F." There he is, in line

as if on a parade ground, between his companions, all alike silent. A little plate of zinc has fallen to his lot, and his name has been patiently stippled, doubtless with the help of a hammer and a nail. His is one of the few graves decked with a wreath, a very modest wreath to be sure, of leaves already discoloured, a token of remembrance from his men who must have loved him, for I know he was gentle with them.

For reference later, when his body will be removed, I am now going to draw a plan of the cemetery in my notebook, counting the rows of graves and the number of graves in each row. Look! bullets are whistling past us, two or three in succession. Whence can they be coming to us, these bullets? They are undoubtedly intended for us, for the noise that each one makes ends in that kind of little honeyed song, "Cooee you! Cooee you!" which is characteristic of them when they expire somewhere in your direction, somewhere quite close. After their flight silence prevails again, but I make more haste with my drawing.

And the longer I remain here the more I am impressed with the horror of the place. Oh this cemetery which, instead of ending like things in real life, plunges little by little into enfolding mists; these tombs, these tombs all decked with gem-like icicles which have dropped as tears drop; the whiteness of the soil, the whiteness of everything, and Death which returns and hovers stealthily, uttering a little cry like a bird! Yonder, by the grave of Pierre D——, I notice Osman, likewise much blurred in the fog. He has found a spade, which has doubtless remained there ever since the interments, and he finishes burying the little bottle which is to serve as a token.

Again that sound, "Cooee you! Cooee

you!" The place is decidedly unhealthy, as the soldiers say. I should be to blame if I lingered here any longer.

Upon my soul, here comes shrapnel! But before I heard it explode in the air I recognised it by the sound of its flight, which is different from that of ordinary shells. This first shot is aimed too far to the right, and the fragments fall twenty or thirty yards away on the little white hillocks. But they have found us out, so much is certain, and that is owing to the microphones. This will continue, and there is no cover anywhere, not a single trench, not a single hole.

"Stoop down, sir, stoop down," shouts Osman from the distance, seeing another coming towards me while my attention is still occupied with the graves. Why should I stoop down? It is a useful precaution against shells. But against shrapnel, which strikes downwards from above?

No, we ought to have our steel helmets, but carelessly, anticipating no danger, we left them in the car with our masks. All that is left for us is to beat a hasty retreat. Osman comes running towards me with his spade and his second little bottle, and I shout at him:

"No, no, it is too late, you must run away."

Good heavens, the car has not even been turned! Why, that was an elementary precaution, and as soon as we arrived I ought to have seen to that. What a long, black record of carelessness to-day; where is my head? It is because our entry to the cemetery was so undisturbed. I call out to the two chauffeurs who were still taking photographs:

"Stop that, stop! Go at once and turn the car! Not too fast though, or you will make too much noise, but hurry up! Run!"

Osman took advantage of this diversion with the chauffeurs to begin digging in the ground near me.

"No, I tell you, stop at once. Can you not see that they are still shelling us? Run and get behind a tree by the roadside."

"But it is all right, sir, it is just finished. It will be finished by the time the car has been turned."

In my heart I am glad that he is disobeying me a little and completing the work. Never was a hole dug so rapidly nor a bottle buried so nimbly. Then he puts back the earth, jumps on it to flatten it down, and throws down his sexton's spade. Then we run away at full speed, stepping on the hillocks of our dead, apologising to them inwardly. Nothing seems so ridiculous and stupid as to run under fire. But I am not alone; the safety of these soldiers is in my charge, and I should be guilty if I delayed them for as much as a second in their flight.

Shrapnel is still bursting, scattering its hail around us. And how strange and subtle are the ways of modern warfare, where death comes thus seeking us out of invisible depths, depths of a horizon that looks like white cotton wool; death launched at us by men whom we can see no more than they can see us, launched blindly, yet in the certainty of finding us.

We reach the car just as it has finished turning; we jump in, and off our car goes at full speed, all open. We pass the occupied trenches like a hurricane; this time heads are scarcely raised because of the shower of shrapnel. These men, to be sure, are under cover, but not so we, who have nothing but our speed to save us.

In our frantic flight, in which my part is simply passive, my imagination is free to return to that gloomy cemetery and its dead. And it was strange how clearly we could hear the shrapnel in the midst of this silence and in this extraordinary mist, which increased, like a microphone, the noise of its flight. It is, moreover, perhaps the first time that I have heard it performing a solo apart from all the customary clamour, in intimacy, if I may say so, for it has done me the honour of coming solely on my account. Never before, then, had I felt that almost physical appreciation of the mad velocity of these little hard bodies, and of the shock with which they must strike against some fragile object, say a chest or a head.

The game is over, and we are entering again the village of B——. Here, out of range of shrapnel, only long-distance guns could reach us. We have not even a broken pane of glass or a scratch. Instinctively the chauffeurs draw up, just as I was about to give the order, not because the car is out of breath, or we either, but we need a moment to regain our composure, to arrange the overcoats thrown into the car in a confused heap, which, after our hurried departure, danced a saraband with cameras, helmets, and revolvers.

And then, like people who at last succeed in finding a shelter from a shower in a gateway, we look at one another and feel inclined to laugh—to laugh in spite of the painful and still recent memory of our dead, to laugh at having made good our escape, to laugh because we have succeeded in doing what we set out to do, and especially because we have defied those imbeciles who were firing at us.

XXIII

THE FIRST SUNSHINE OF MARCH

March 10th, 1916.

It is just here, I believe, that that zone, some fifteen to twenty miles in breadth, so terribly torn and rent, which stretches through our land of France from the North Sea to Alsace, following the line of those trenches, where the barbarians have dug themselves in, it is just here, I believe, that that zone, where suffering and glory reign supreme, attains the climax of its nightmare-like illusiveness, the climax of its horror. I say "just here" because I am not allowed to be more definite; just here, however, in a certain province which had even before the war a depressing nickname, something like "the desolate province," "the mean province," or even, if you like, "the lousy province." The reason was that even before it was laid waste it was already very barren, almost without verdure; it had nothing to show except unfruitful valleys, some clumps of stunted pines, some poverty-stricken villages, which had not even the saving grace of antiquity, for century by century savages from Germany had come and disported themselves there, and when they went away everything had to be rebuilt.

And now since the great new onrush, which surpassed all abominations ever before experienced, how strange, fantastic almost, seems this region of woe, with its calcined ruins, its chalky soil dug over and again dug over down to its very depths, as if by myriads of burrowing animals.

Once again I make my way to-day in my motor car into the midst of it all on some mission assigned to me, and I had never yet seen it in all the mire of the thaw, in which our poor little warriors in blue caps are so uncomfortably engulfed up to midleg. I feel my heart sinking more and more the farther I go along these broken-up roads, which are becoming still more crowded with our dear soldiers, all lamentably coated with greyish mud. The occasional villages on our road are more and more damaged by shells, and peasant women or children are no longer to be seen; there are no more civilians, nothing but blue helmets, but of these there are thousands. The rapid melting of the snow in such a sudden burst of sunshine marks the distant landscape with zebra-like stripes, white and earth-coloured. And all the hills which we pass now seem to be inhabited by tribes of troglodytes, while every slope which faces us, who are coming in this direction, and which, owing to its position, has thus escaped the notice and the fire of the enemy, is riddled with mouths of caves, some ranged in rows, some built in stories one above the other, and from these peer out human heads in helmets, enjoying the sun. What can this country be? Is it prehistoric, or merely very remote? Surely no one would say that it was France. Save for this bitter, icy wind, this country, with its sky almost too blue to-day for a northern sky, might be taken for the banks of the upper Nile, the Libyan ridge where subterranean caverns gape.

Again a semblance of a village appears, the last through which I shall pass, for those which are distant landmarks on the road that leads towards the barbarians, are nothing more now than hapless heaps of stone resembling barrows. This village, too, be it understood, is three-quarters in ruins; there remain fragments of walls in grotesque shapes, letting in the daylight and displaying a black marbling of soot where the chimneys used to be. But many soldiers are gaily having their breakfast in the purely imaginary shelter afforded them by these remains of houses. There are pay-sergeants even, who are seated unconcernedly at improvised tables, busy with their writing.

Bang! A shell! It is a shell hurled blindly and from a great distance by the barbarians, without definite purpose, merely in the hope that it may succeed in hurting someone. It has fallen on the ruins of a roofless stable, where some poor horses are tethered, and here are two of them who have been struck down and are lying bellies upwards and kicking out, as they do when they are dying; they stain the snow crimson with blood spurting from their chests in jets, as if forced from a pump.

The village soon disappears in the distance, and I enter this no man's land, always rather a solemn region, which from end to end along the front indicates the immediate neighbourhood of the barbarians. The March sun, astonishingly strong, beats down upon this tragic desert where great sheets of white snow alternate with broad, mud-coloured surfaces. And now whenever my car stops and pauses, for some reason or other, and the engine is silent, the noise of the cannon is heard more and more loudly.

At last I reach the farthest point to which my car can convey me; if I took it on farther it would be seen by the Boches, and the shells that are roaming about here and there in the air would converge upon it. It must be safely bestowed, together with my chauffeurs, in a hollow of the undulating ground, while I continue my journey alone on foot.

First of all I have to telephone to General Headquarters. The telephone office is that dark hole over there, hidden among scanty bushes. Climbing down a very narrow flight of steps, I penetrate seven or eight yards into the earth, and there I find four soldiers installed as telephone girls, illumined by tiny electric lamps that shine like glow-worms. These are territorials, about forty years of age, and the man who hands me the telephone apparatus wears a wedding ring—doubtless he has a wife and children living somewhere yonder out in the open air, where life is possible. Nevertheless he tells me that he has been six months in this damp hole, beneath the surface of ground which is continually swept by shells, and he tells me this with cheerful resignation, as if the sacrifice were quite a natural thing. In the same spirit his companions speak of their white-ant existence without a shade of complaint. And these, too, are worthy of admiration, all these patient heroes of the darkness, equally so, perhaps, with their comrades who fight in the open air in the light of day, with mutual encouragement.

Emerging from the underground cave, where the noises are muffled, I hear very clearly the cannonade; my eyes are dazzled by the unwonted sunlight which illumines all those white stretches of snow.

I have to journey about two miles through this strange desert to reach a paltry little clump of sorry-looking pines which I perceive over there on some rising ground. It is there that I have made an appointment to meet an officer of sappers, whom my business concerns, for the purpose of fulfilling my mission.

A pretence of a desert, I ought rather to call it, for underground it is thickly populated by our soldiers, armed and alert. At the first signal of an attack they would rush out through a thousand apertures; but for the moment, throughout the whole extent of this tract, so sun-steeped and yet so cold, not more than one or two blue caps are visible, belonging to men who are stealing along from one shelter to another.

And it is, moreover, a terribly noisy desert, for besides the continual detonation of artillery from varying ranges, there is a noise like huge kinds of beetles flying, which, as they pass, make almost the same buzzing sound as aeroplanes, but they all fly so fast as to be invisible. Their flight is haphazard, and when they strike their heads hard against the ground pebbles, earth, scrap-iron, spout up in jets shaped like wheat-sheaves. On the eastern horizon, silhouetted against the sky, stands one of those tumuli of ruins which now mark the place of former villages; and it is here especially that those huge beetles are bent on falling, raising each time clouds of plaster and dust. It is, to be sure, a useless and idle bombardment, for already all this has perished.

To-day especially, being a day of a great thaw, a distance of two miles here in this region where so many of our poor soldiers are doomed to exist, is equal to a distance of at least ten miles elsewhere—it is such heavy going. You sink up to your ankles in mud, and you cannot draw your foot out, for the mud sticks tight like glue. The wind still remains cold and icy, but in the midst of a sky too deeply blue shines a sun, beating down upon my head, and under the steel helmet, which grows heavier and heavier, beads of sweat stand upon my forehead. The snow has made up its mind to melt, and that suddenly. All the summits of those melancholy-looking hills, bared of their covering, resume again their brown colour and resemble hindquarters of animals couching on these plains which still remain white.

This is the first time that I find myself absolutely, infinitely alone, in the midst of this scene of intense desolation, which, though to-day it happens to glitter with light, is none the less dismal. Until I reach the little wood whither I am bound on duty there is nothing to think about, nothing with which I need concern myself. I need not trouble to get out of the way of shells, for they would not give me time, nor even to select places where to put my feet, since I sink in equally wherever I step. And so, gradually, I find myself relapsing into a state of mind characteristic of former days before the war, and I look at all these things to which I had grown accustomed and view them impartially, as if they were new. Twenty short months ago, who would have imagined such scenes? For instance, these countless spoil-heaps, white in colour, because the soil of this province is white, spoil-heaps which are thrown up everywhere in long lines, tracing on the desert so many zebra-like stripes; is it possible that these indicate the only tracks by which to-day our soldiers of France can move about with some measure of safety? They are little hollow tracks, some undulating, some straight, communication trenches which the French nickname "intestines." These have been multiplied again and again, until the ground is furrowed with them unendingly. What prodigious work, moreover, they represent, these mole-like paths, spreading like a network over hundreds of leagues. If to their sum be added trenches, shelter caves, and all those catacombs that penetrate right into the heart of the hills, the mind is amazed at excavations so extensive, which would seem the work of centuries.

And these strange kinds of nets, stretched out in all directions, would anyone, unless previously warned and accustomed to them, understand what they were? They look as if gigantic spiders had woven their webs around countless numbers of posts, which stretch out beyond range of sight, some in straight lines, some in circles or crescents, tracing on that wide tract of country designs in which there must surely be some cabalistic significance intended to envelop and entangle the barbarians more effectively. Since I last came this way these obstructing nets must have been reinforced to a terrible extent, and their number has been multiplied by two, by ten. In order to achieve such inextricable confusion our soldiers, those weavers of snares, must have made in them turnings and twists with their great bobbins of barbed wire carried under their arms. But here, at various points, are enclosures, whose purpose is obvious at a glance and which add to the grisly horror of the whole scene; these fences of wood surround closely packed groups of humble little wooden crosses made of two sticks. Alas! what they are is clear at first sight. Thus, then, they lie, within sound of the cannonade, as if the battle were not yet over for them, these dear comrades of ours who have vanished, heroes humble yet sublime—inapproachable for the present, even for those who weep for them, inapproachable, because death never ceases to fly through the air which stirs overhead, above their little silent gatherings.

Ah! to complete the impression of unreality a black bird appears of fabulous size, a monster of the Apocalypse, flying with great clamour aloft in the air. He is moving in the direction of France, seeking, no doubt, some more sheltered region, where at last women and children are to be found, in the hope of destroying some of them. I keep on walking, if walking it can be called, this wearisome, pitiless repetition of plunges into snow and ice-cold mud. At last I reach the clump of trees where we have arranged to meet. I am thankful to have arrived there, for my helmet and cap were encumbrances under that unexpectedly hot sun. I am, however, before my time. The officer whom I invited to meet me here—in order to discuss questions concerning new works of defence, new networks of lines, new pits—that is he, no doubt, that blue silhouette coming this way across the snow-shrouded ground. But he is far away, and for a few more moments I can still indulge in the reverie with which I whiled away the journey, before the time comes when I must once more become precise and businesslike. Evidently the place is not one of perfect peace, for it is clear that these melancholy boughs, half stripped of leaves already, have suffered from those great humming cockchafers that fly across from time to time, and have been shot through as if they were no stronger than sheets of paper. It is, to be sure, but a small wood, yet it keeps me company, wrapping me round with an illusion of safety.

I am standing here on rising ground, where the wind blows more icily, and I command a view of the whole terrible landscape, a succession of monotonous hills, striped in zebra fashion with whitish trenches; its few trees have been blasted by shrapnel. In the distance that network of iron wire, stretching out in all directions, shines brightly in the sun, and is not unlike the gossamer which floats over the meadows in spring time. And on all sides the detonation of artillery continues with its customary clamour, unceasing here, day and night, like the sea beating against the cliffs.

Ah! the big black bird has found someone to talk to in the air. I see it suddenly assailed by a quantity of those flakes of white cotton wool (bursts of shrapnel), in appearance so innocent, yet so dangerous to birds of his feather. So he hurriedly turns back, and his crimes are postponed to another day.

From behind a neighbouring hill issues a squad of men in blue, who will reach me before the officer on the road yonder. It is one, just one, of a thousand of those little processions which, alas! may be met with every hour all along the front, forming, as it were, part of the scenery. In front march four soldiers carrying a stretcher, and others follow them to relieve them. They, too, are attracted by the delusive hope of protection afforded by the branches, and at the beginning of the wood they stop instinctively for a breathing space and to change shoulders. They have come from first line trenches a

WAR

mile or two away and are carrying a seriously wounded man to a subterranean field hospital, not more than a quarter of an hour's walk away. They, likewise, had not anticipated the heat of that terrible March sun, which is beating down on their heads; they are wearing their helmets and winter caps, and these weigh upon them as heavily as the precious burden which they are so careful not to jolt. In addition to this they drag along on each leg a thick crust of snow and sticky mud, which makes their feet as heavy as elephants' feet, and the sweat pours in great drops down their faces, cheerful in spite of fatigue.

"Where is your man wounded?" I ask, in a low voice.

In a voice still lower comes the reply: "His stomach is ripped open, and the Major in the trench said that——" they finish the sentence merely by shaking their heads, but I have understood. Besides he has not stirred. His poor hand remains lying across his eyes and forehead, doubtless to protect them from the burning sun, and I ask them:

"Why have you not covered his face?"

"We put a handkerchief over it, sir, but he took it off. He said he preferred to remain like this, *so that he could still look at things between his fingers.*"

Ah! the last two men have blood as well as sweat pouring over their faces and trickling in a little stream down their necks.

"It is nothing much, sir," they say, "we got that as soon as we started. We began by carrying him along the communication trenches, but that jolted him too much, so then we walked along outside in the open."

Poor fellows, admirable for their very carelessness. To save their wounded man from jolts they risked their own lives.

Two or three of these death-bringing cockchafers, which go humming along here at all hours, came down and were crushed to pieces on the stones close to them, and wounded them with their shattered fragments. The Germans disdain to fire at a single wayfarer like myself, but a group of men, and a stretcher in particular, they cannot resist. One of these men, both of whom are dripping with blood, has perhaps actually received only a scratch, but the other has lost an ear; only a shred is left, hanging by a thread.

"You must go at once and have your wound dressed at the hospital, my friend," I say to him.

"Yes, sir. And we are just on our way there, to the hospital. It is very lucky."

This is the only idea of complaint that has entered his head.

"It is very lucky."

And he says this with such a quiet, pleasant smile, grateful to me for taking an interest in him.

I hesitated before going to look more closely at their seriously wounded man who never stirred, for I feared lest I should disturb his last dream. Nevertheless I approach him very gently, because they are just going to carry him away.

Alas! he is almost a child, a child from some village; so much is clear from his bronzed cheeks, which have scarcely yet begun to turn pale. The sun, even as he desired, shines full upon his comely face, the face of a boy of twenty, with a frank and energetic expression, and his hand still shades his eyes, which have a fixed look and seem to have done with sight. Some morphia had to be given him to spare him at least unnecessary suffering.

Lowly child of our peasantry, little ephemeral being, of what is he dreaming, if indeed he still dreams? Perhaps of a white-capped mother who wept tender tears whenever she recognised his childish writing on an envelope from the front. Or perhaps he is dreaming of a cottage garden, the delight of his earliest years, where, he reflects, this warm March sun will call to life new shoots all along some old wall. On his chest I see the handkerchief with which one of the men had attempted to cover his face; it is a fine handkerchief, embroidered with a marquis's coronet—the coronet of one of his stretcher bearers. He had desired *still to look at things,* in his terror, doubtless, of the black night. But soon he will suddenly cease to be aware of this same sun, which now must dazzle him. First of all he will enter the half-darkness of the field hospital, and immediately afterwards there will descend upon him that black inexorable night, in which no March sun will ever rise again.

"Go on at once, my friends," I say to

them, "the wind blows too cold here for people drenched with sweat like you."

I watch them move away, their legs weighted with slabs of viscous mud. My admiration and my compassion go with them on their way through the snow, where they plod along so laboriously.

These men, to be sure, still have some privileges, for they can at least help one another, and careful hands are waiting to dress their wounds in an underground refuge, which is almost safe. But close to this, at Verdun, there are thousands of others, who have fallen in confused heaps, smothering one another. Underneath corpses lie dying men, whom it is impossible to rescue from those vast charnel-houses, so long ago and so scientifically prepared by the Kaiser for the greater glory of that ferocious young nonentity whom he has for a son.

XXIV

AT SOISSONS

September, 1915.

Soissons is one of our great martyred towns of the north; it can be entered only by circuitous and secret paths, with such precautions as Redskins take in a forest, for the barbarians are hidden everywhere within the earth and on the hill close at hand, and with field-glasses at their wicked eyes they scan the roads, so that they may shower shrapnel on any rash enough to approach that way.

One delightful September evening I was guided towards this town by some officers accustomed to its dangerous surroundings. Taking a zigzag course over low-lying ground, through deserted gardens, where the last roses of the season bloomed and the trees were laden with fruit, we reached without accident the suburbs, and were soon actually in the streets of the town. Grass had already begun to sprout there from the ruins during the last year in which all signs of human life had vanished. From time to time we met some groups of soldiers, otherwise not a soul, and a death-like silence held sway under that wonderful late-summer sky.

Before the invasion it was one of these towns, fallen a little into neglect, that exist in the depths of our provinces of France, with modest mansions displaying armorial bearings and standing in little squares planted with elms; and life there must have been very peaceful in the midst of somewhat old-fashioned ways and customs. It is in the destruction of these old hereditary homes, which were doubtless loved and venerated, that senseless barbarism daily wreaks its vengeance. Many of these buildings have collapsed, scattering on to the pavement their antiquated furniture, and in their present immobility remain, as it were, in postures of suffering. This evening there happens to be a lull. A few somewhat distant cannon shots still come and punctuate, if I may say so, the funereal monotony of the hours; but this intermittent music is so customary in these parts that though it is heard it attracts no notice. Instead of disturbing the silence, it seems actually to emphasise it and at the same time to deepen its tragedy.

Here and there, on walls that still remain undamaged, little placards are posted, printed on white paper, with the notice: "House still occupied." Underneath, written by hand, are the names of the pertinacious occupants, and somehow, I cannot say why, this strikes the observer as being a rather futile formality. Is it to keep away robbers or to warn off shells?

And where else, in what scene of desolation similar to this, have I noticed before other little placards such as these? Ah, I remember! It was at Pekin, during its occupation by European troops, in that unhappy quarter which fell into the hands of Germany, where the Kaiser's soldiers gave rein to all their worst instincts, for they may be judged on that occasion, those brutes, by comparing their conduct with that of the soldiers of the other allied countries, who occupied the adjoining quarters of the town without harming anyone. No, the Germans, they alone practised torture, and the poor creatures delivered up to their doltish cruelty tried to preserve themselves by pasting on their doors ingenuous inscriptions such as these, "Here dwell Chinese under French protection," or "All who dwell here are Chinese Christians." But this availed them nothing. Besides, their Emperor—

the same, always the same, who is sure to be lurking, his tentacles swollen with blood, at the bottom of every gaping wound in whatever country of the world, the same great organiser of slaughter on earth, lord of trickery, prince of shambles and of charnel-houses—he himself had said to his troops:

"Go and do as the Huns did. Let China remain for a century terrorised by your visitation."

And they all obeyed him to the letter.

But the treasures out of those houses in Pekin, pillaged by his orders, that lay strewn on the ancient paving-stones of the streets over there, were quantities of relics very strange to us, very unfamiliar —images sacred to Chinese worship, fragments of altars dedicated to ancestors, little *stelae* of lacquer, on which were inscribed in columns long genealogies of Manchus whose origins were lost in night.

Here, on the other hand, in this town as it is this evening, the poor household gods that lie among the ruins are objects familiar to us, and the sight of them wrings our hearts even more. There is a child's cradle, a humble piano of antiquated design, which has fallen upside down from an upper story, and still conjures up the thought of old sonatas played of an evening in the family circle.

And I remember to have seen, lying in the filth of a gutter, a photograph reverently "enlarged" and framed, the portrait of a charming old grandmother, with her hair in curl-papers. She must have been long at rest in some burial vault, and doubtless the desecrated portrait was the last earthly likeness of her that still survived.

The noise of the cannon comes nearer as we move on through these streets in their death-agony, where, during a whole summer of desolation, grasses and wild flowers have had time to spring up.

In the midst of the town stands a cathedral, a little older than that of Rheims and very famous in the history of France. The Germans, to be sure, delighted in making it their target, always under the same pretext, with a stupid attempt at cleverness, that there was an observation post at the top of the towers. A priest in a cassock bordered with red, who has never fled from the shells, opens the door for us and accompanies us.

It is a very startling surprise to find on entering that the interior of the church is white throughout with the glaring whiteness of a perfectly new building. In spite of the breaches which the barbarians have made in the walls from top to bottom, it does not, at first sight, resemble a ruin, but rather a building in course of construction, a work which is still proceeding. It is, moreover, a miracle of strength and grace, a masterpiece of our Gothic Art in the matchless purity of its first bloom.

The priest explains to us the reason for this disconcerting whiteness. Before the coming of the barbarians, the long task was scarcely completed of exposing the under-surface of each stone in turn, so that the joints might be more carefully repaired with cement; thus the grey hue with which the church had been encrusted by the smoke of incense, burnt there for so many centuries, had resolved itself into dust. It was perhaps rather sacrilegious, this scraping away of the surface, but I believe it helps to a better appreciation of the architectural beauties. Indeed, under that unvarying shade of cinder-grey which we are accustomed to find in our old churches, the slender pillars, the delicate groining of the vaults, seem, as it were, made all in one, and it might be imagined that no skill had been necessary to cause them thus to soar upwards. Here, on the contrary, it is incomprehensible, disconcerting almost, to see how these myriads and myriads of little stones, so distinct each from the other in their renovated setting, remain thus suspended, forming a ceiling at such a height above our heads. Far better than in churches blurred with smoky grey is revealed the patient, miraculous labour of those artists of old, who, without the help of our iron-work or our modern contrivances, succeeded in bestowing stability upon things so fragile and ethereal.

Within the basilica, as without, prevails an anguished silence, punctuated slowly by the noise of cannon shots. And on the episcopal throne this device remains legible, which, in the midst of such ruin, has the force of an ironic anathema launched against the barbarians, *pax et justitia*.

Walking among the scattered *débris,* I pick my way as carefully as possible to avoid stepping on precious fragments of stained-glass windows; it is pleasanter not to hear underfoot the little tinkle of breaking glass. All the shades of light of the summer evening, seldom seen in such sanctuaries, stream in through gaping rents, or through beautiful thirteenth-century windows, now but hollow frameworks. And the double row of columns vanishes in perspective in the luminous white atmosphere like a forest of gigantic white reeds planted in line.

Emerging from the cathedral, in one of the deserted streets, we come upon a wall covered with printed placards, which the shells seem to have been at special pains to tear. These placards were placed side by side as close together as possible, the margins of each encroaching upon those of its neighbours, as if jealous of the space the others occupied and all with an appearance of wishing to cover up and to devour one another. In spite of the shrapnel which has riddled them so effectively, some passages are still legible, doubtless those that were considered essential, printed as they were in much larger letters so that they might better strike the eye.

"Treason! Scandalous bluff!" shouts one of the posters.

"Infamous slander! Base lie!" replies the other, in enormous, arresting letters.

What on earth can all this mean?

Ah yes, it is a manifestation of all the pettiness of our last little election contests which has remained placarded here, pilloried as it were, still legible in spite of the rains of two summers and the snows of one winter. It is surprising how these absurdities have survived, simply on scraps of paper pasted on the walls of houses. As a rule no wayfarer looks at such things as he passes them, for in our day they have become too contemptible for a smile or a shrug of the shoulders. But on this wall, where the shells have ironically treated them as they deserved, piercing them with a thousand holes, they suddenly assume, I know not why, an air irresistibly and indescribably comic; we owe them a moment of relaxation and hearty laughter—it is doubtless the only time in their miserable little existence that they have at least served some purpose.

To-day who indeed remembers the scurrilities of the past? They who wrote them and who perhaps even now are brothers-in-arms, fighting side by side, would be the first to laugh at them. I will not say that later on, when the barbarians have at last gone away, party spirit will not again, here and there, attempt to raise its head. But none the less in this great war it has received a blow from which it will never recover. Whatever the future may hold for us, nothing can alter the fact that once in France, from end to end of our battle front and during long months, there were these interlacing networks of little tunnels called trenches. And these trenches, which seemed at first sight nothing but horrible pits of sordid misery and suffering, will actually have been the grandest of our temples, where we all came together to be purified and to communicate, as it were, at the same holy table.

As for our trenches, they begin close at hand, too close alas! to the martyred town; there they are, in the midst of the mall, and we make our way thither through these desolate streets where there is no one to be seen.

Everyone knows that almost all our provincial towns have their mall, a shady avenue of trees often centuries old; this one was reputed to be among the finest in

France. But it is indeed too risky to venture there, for death is ever prowling about and we can only cross it furtively by these tortuous tunnels, hastily excavated, which are called communication trenches.

First of all we are shown a comprehensive view of the mall through a loophole in a thick wall. Its melancholy is even more poignant than that of the streets, because this was once a favourite spot where formerly the good people of the town used to resort for relaxation and quiet gaiety. It stretches away out of sight between its two rows of elms. It is empty, to be sure, empty and silent. A funereal growth of grass carpets its long alleys with verdure, as if it were given up to the peace of a lasting abandonment, and in this exquisite evening hour the setting sun traces there row upon row of golden lines, reaching away into the distance among the lengthening shadows of the trees. It might be deemed empty indeed, the mall of this martyred town, where at this moment nothing stirs, nothing is heard. But here and there it is furrowed with upturned earth, resembling, on a large scale, those heaps that rats and moles throw up in the fields. Now we can guess the meaning of this, for we are well acquainted with the system of clandestine passages used in modern warfare. From these ominous little excavations we conclude at once that, contrary to expectations, this place of mournful silence is populated by a terrible race of men concealed beneath its green grass; that eager eyes survey it from all sides, that hidden cannon cover it, that it needs but an imperceptible signal to cause a furious manifestation of life to burst forth there out of the ground, with fire and blood and shouts and all the clamour of death.

And now by means of a narrow, carefully hidden descent we penetrate into those paths termed communication trenches, which will bring us close, quite close, to the barbarians, so close that we shall almost hear them breathe. A walk along those trenches is a somewhat unpleasant experience and seems interminable. The atmosphere is hot and heavy; you labour under the impression that people are pressing upon you too closely, and that your shoulders will rub against the earthen walls; and then at every ten or twelve paces there are little bends, intentionally abrupt, which force you to turn in your own ground; you are conscious of having walked ten times the distance and of having advanced scarcely at all. How great is the temptation to scale the parapet which borders the trench in order to reach the open air, or merely to put one's head above it to see at least in which direc-

tion the path tends. But to do so would
be certain death. And indeed there is
something torturing in this sense of im-
prisonment within this long labyrinth, and
in the knowledge that in order to escape
from it alive there is no help for it, but
to retrace one's steps along that vague succession of little turnings, strangling and
obstructing.

The heat and oppressiveness of the
atmosphere in these tunnels is increased
by the number of persons to be met there,
men in horizon blue overcoats, flattening
themselves against the wall, whom, nevertheless, the visitor brushes against as he
passes. In some parts the trenches are
crowded like the galleries of an ant-hill,
and if it suddenly became necessary to take
flight, what a scene would ensue of confusion and crushing. To be sure the faces
of these men are so smiling and at the
same time so resolute that the idea of

their flight from any danger whatsoever does not even enter the mind.

As the hour for their evening meal approaches they begin to set up their little tables, here and there, in the safest corners, in shelters with vaulted roofs. Obviously it is necessary to have supper early in order to be able to see, for certainly no lamps will be lighted. At nightfall it will be as dark here as in hell, and unless there is an alarm, an attack with sudden and flashing lights, they will have to feel their way about until to-morrow morning.

Here comes a cheerful procession of men carrying soup. The soup has been rather long on the way through these winding paths, but it is still hot and has a pleasant fragrance, and the messmates sit down, or get as near to that attitude as they can. What a strangely assorted company, and yet on what good terms they seem to be! To-day I have no time to linger, but I re-

WAR 283

member lately sitting a long time and chatting at the end of a meal in a trench in the Argonne. Of that company, seated side by side, one was formerly a long-named conscientious objector, turned now into a heroic sergeant, whose eyes will actually grow misty with tears at the sight of one of our bullet-pierced flags borne along. Near him sat a former *apache,* whose cheeks, once pale from nights spent in squalid drinking-kens, were now bronzed by the open air, and he seemed at present a decent little fellow; and finally, the gayest of them all was a fine-looking soldier of about thirty, who no longer had time to shave his long beard, but nevertheless preserved carefully a tonsure on the top of his head. And the comrade, who every other day did his best to conserve this tell-tale manner of hairdressing, was formerly a root-and-branch anticlericalist, by profession a zinc-maker at Belleville.

We continue our way, still without seeing anything, following blindly. But we must be near the end of our journey, for we are told:

"Now you must walk without making a sound and speak softly," and a little farther on, "Now you must not speak at all."

And when one of us raises his head too high a sharp report rings out close to us, and a bullet whistles over our heads, misses its mark, and is lost in the brushwood, whence it strips the leaves. Afterwards silence falls again, more profound, stranger than ever.

The terminus is a vaulted redoubt, its walls composed partly of clay, partly of sheet-iron. This blindage has been pierced with two or three little holes, which can be very quickly opened or shut by rapidly working mechanism, and it is through these holes alone that it is possible for us to look out for a few seconds with some measure of safety, without receiving suddenly a bullet in the head by way of the eyes.

What, have we only come as far as this? After walking all this time we have not reached even the end of the mall. In front of us still extend, under the shade of the elms, straight and peaceful, its desolate grass-grown walks. The sun has blotted out the golden lines it was tracing a moment ago, and twilight will presently be over all, and there is still no sound, not even the cries of birds calling one another home to roost; it is like the immobility and silence of death.

Looking in a different direction through another opening in the sheet-iron, on the other bank (the right bank), scarcely twenty yards away from us, quite close to the edge of the little river, of which we hold the left bank, we notice perfectly new earth-works, masked by the kindly protection of branches, and there, as in the mall, silence prevails, but it is the same silence, too obviously studied, suspicious, full of dread. Then someone whispers in my ear:

"It is *They* who are there."

It is *They* who are there, as indeed we had surmised, for in many other places we had already observed similar dreadful regions, close to our own, steeped in a deceptive silence, characteristic of ultra-modern warfare. Yes, it is *They* who are there, still there, well entrenched in the shelter of our own French soil, which does not even fall in upon them and smother them. Sons of that vile race which has the taint of lying in its blood, they have taught all the armies of the world the art of making even inanimate objects lie, even the outward semblance of things. Their trenches under their verdure disguise themselves as innocent furrows; the houses that shelter their staffs assume the aspect of deserted ruins. They are never to be seen, these hidden enemies; they advance and invade like white ants or gnawing worms, and then at the most unexpected moment of day or night, preceded by all varieties of diabolical preparations that they have devised, burning liquids, blinding gas, asphyxiating gas, they leap out from the ground like beasts in a menagerie whose cages have been unfastened. How humiliating! After prodigious efforts in mechanics and chemistry to revert to the custom of the age of cave-dwellers; after fighting for more than a year with lethal weapons perfected with infernal ingenuity for slaughter at long range to be found thus, almost on top of one another for months at a time, with straining nerves and every sense alert, and yet all hidden away under cover, not daring to budge an inch!

How horrible! I believe they were actually whispering in those trenches opposite. Like ourselves they speak in low voices; nevertheless the German intonation is unmistakable. They are talking to one another, those invisible beings. In the infinite silence that surrounds us, their muffled whispers come to us, as it were, from below, from the bowels of the earth. An abrupt command, doubtless uttered by one of their officers, calls them to order, and they are suddenly silent. But we have heard them, heard them close to us, and that murmur, proceeding, as it were, from burrowing animals, falls more mournfully upon the ear than any clamour of battle.

It is not that their voices were brutal; on the contrary, they sounded almost musical, so much so that had we not known who the talkers were we should not have felt that shudder of disgust pass through our flesh; we should have been inclined, rather, to say to them:

"Come, a truce to this game of death! Are we not men and brothers? Come out of your shelters and let us shake hands."

But it is only too well known that if their voices are human and their faces too, more or less, it is not so with their souls. They lack the vital moral senses, loyalty, honour, remorse, and that sentiment especially, which is perhaps noblest of all and yet most elementary, which even animals sometimes possess, the sentiment of pity.

I remember a phrase of Victor Hugo which formerly seemed to me exaggerated and obscure; he said:

"Night, which in a wild beast takes the place of a soul."

To-day, thanks to the revelation of the German soul, I understand the metaphor. What else can there be but impenetrable, rayless night in the soul of their baleful

Emperor and in the soul of their heir apparent, his ferret face dwarfed by a black busby with the charming adornment of a death's head? All their lives they have had no other thought than to construct engines for slaughter, to invent explosives and poisons for slaughter, to train soldiers for slaughter. For the sake of their monstrous personal vanity they organised all the barbarism latent in the depths of the German race; they organised (I repeat the word because though it is not good French alas! it is essentially German), they "organised," then, its indigenous ferocity; organised its grotesque megalomania; organised its sheep-like submissiveness and imbecile credulity. And afterwards they did not die of horror at the sight of their own work! Can it be that they still dare to go on living, these creatures of darkness? In the sight of so many tears, so many torments, such vast ossuaries, that infamous pair continue peacefully sleeping, eating, receiving homage, and doubtless they will pose for sculptors and be immortalised in bronze or marble—all this when they ought to be subjected to a refinement of old Chinese tortures. Oh, all this that I say about them is not for the sake of uselessly stirring up the hatred of the world; no, but I believe it to be my duty to do all that in me lies to arrest that perilous forgetfulness which will once again shut its eyes to their crimes. So much do I fear our light-hearted French ways, our simple, confiding disposition. We are quite capable of allowing the tentacles of the great devil-fish gradually to worm their way again into our flesh. Who knows if our country will not soon be swarming again with a vermin of countless spies, crafty parasites, navvies working clandestinely at concrete platforms for German cannon under the very floors of our dwellings. Oh, let us never forget that this predatory race is incurably treacherous, thievish, murderous; that no treaty of peace will ever bind it, and that until it is crushed, until its head has been cut off—its terrible Gorgon head which is Prussian Imperialism—it will always begin again.

When in the streets of our towns we meet those young men who are disabled, mutilated, who walk along slowly in groups, supporting one another, or those young men who are blinded and are led by the hand, and all those women, bowed down, as it were, under their veils of crape, let us reflect:

"This is their work. And the man who spent so long a time preparing all this for us is their Kaiser—and he, if he be not crushed, will think of nothing but how he may begin all over again to-morrow."

And outside railway stations where men

are entrained for the front, we may meet some young woman with a little child in her arms, restraining the tears that stand in her brave, sorrowful eyes, who has come to say good-bye to a soldier in field kit. At the sight of her let us say to ourselves:

"This man, whose return is so passionately longed for, the Kaiser's shrapnel doubtless awaits; to-morrow he may be hurled, nameless, among thousands of others, into those charnel-houses in which Germany delights, and which she will ask nothing better than to be allowed to begin filling again."

Especially when we see passing by in their new blue uniforms the "young class," our dearly loved sons, who march away so splendidly with pride and joy in their boyish eyes, with bunches of roses at the ends of their rifles, let us consider well our holy vengeance against the enemy who are lying in wait for them yonder—

and against the great Accursed, whose soul is black as night.

From that roofed-over redoubt where we are at present, whose iron flaps we have to raise if we would look out, the mall is still visible with its green grass; the mall, lying there so peaceful in the dim light of evening. The barbarians are no more to be heard; they have stopped talking; they do not move or breathe; and only a sense of uneasy sadness, I had almost said of discouraged sadness, remains, at the thought that they are so near.

But in order to be restored to hope and cheerful confidence, it is sufficient to turn back along the communication trenches, where the men are just finishing their supper in the pleasant twilight. As soon as our soldiers are far enough away from those others to talk freely and laugh freely, there is suddenly a wave of healthy gaiety and of perfect and reassuring confidence.

Here is the true fountain-head of our irresistible strength; from this source we draw that marvellous energy which characterises our attacks and will secure the final victory. Very striking at first sight in the groups around these tables is the excellent understanding, a kind of affectionate familiarity, that unites officers and men. For a long time this spirit has existed in the Navy, where protracted exile from home and dangers shared in the close association of life on board ship necessarily draw men nearer together; but I do not think my comrades of the land forces will be angry with me if I say that this familiarity, so compatible with discipline, is a more recent development with them than with us. One of the benefits conferred upon them by trench warfare is the necessity of living thus nearer to their soldiers, and this gives them an opportunity of winning their affection. At present they know nearly all those comrades of theirs who are simple privates; they call them by name and talk to them like friends. And so, when the solemn moment comes for the attack, when, instead of driving them in front of them with whips, after the fashion of the savages over there, they lead them, after the manner of the French, it is hardly necessary for them to turn round to see if everyone is following them.

Moreover, they are very sure that, if they fall, their humble comrades will not fail to hasten to their side, and, at the risk of their own lives, defend them, or carry them tenderly away.

Now it is to this superhuman war, and especially to the common existence in the trenches, that we owe the ennobling influence of this concord, those sublime acts of mutual devotion, at which we are tempted to bend the knee. And in part is it not likewise owing to life in the trenches, to long and more intimate conversations between officers and men, that these gleams of beauty have penetrated into the minds of all, even of those whose intelligence seemed in the last degree unimpressionable and jaded. They know now, our soldiers, even the least of them, that France has never been so worthy of admiration, and that its glory casts a light upon them all. They know that a race is imperishable in which the hearts of all awaken thus to life, and that Neutral Countries, even those whose eyes seem blinded by the most impenetrable scales, will in the end see clearly and bestow upon us the glorious name of liberators.

Oh let us bless these trenches of ours, where all ranks of society intermingle, where friendships have been formed which yesterday would not have seemed possible, where men of the world will have learnt that the soul of a peasant, an artisan, a common workman may prove itself as great and good as that of a very fine gentleman, and of even deeper interest, being more impulsive, more transparent and with less veneer upon it.

In trenches, communication trenches, little dark labyrinths, little tunnels where men suffer and sacrifice themselves, there will be found established our best and purest school of socialism. But by this term socialism, a term too often profaned, I mean true socialism, be it understood, which is synonymous with tolerance and brotherhood, that socialism, in a word, which Christ came to teach us in that clear formula, which in its adorable simplicity sums up all formulæ, "Love one another."

XXV

THE TWO GORGON HEADS

"My plan is first to take possession. At a later stage I can always find learned men to prove that I was acting within my just rights."

FREDERICK II.

(called, for want of a better epithet, the Great).

I

THEIR KAISER

April, 1916.

There are certain faces of the accursed, which reveal in the end with the coming of old age the accumulated horror and darkness that has been seething in the depths of the soul. The features are by no means always ignoble, but on these faces something is imprinted which is a thousand times worse than ugliness, and none can bear to look upon them. Thus it is with their Kaiser. The sight of his sinister presentment alone, a mere glimpse of the smallest portrait of him reproduced in a newspaper, is sufficient to make the blood run cold. Oh that viperine eye of his, shaded by flaccid lids, that smile twisted awry by all his secret vices, his utter hypocrisy, morbid brutality, added to cold ferocity, and overweening arrogance which in itself is enough to provoke a horsewhip to lash him of its own accord. Once in an old temple in Japan I saw a gruesome work of art, which was considered a masterpiece of genre painting, and had been preserved for centuries, wrapped in a veil, in one of the coffers containing temple treasures.

It is well known how highly the Japanese esteem gruesome works of art, and what masters their artists are in the cult of the horrible. It was a mask of a human face, with features, if anything, rather regular and refined, but if you looked at it attentively its appalling expression, at the same time cruel and lifeless, haunted you for days and nights. From out the cadaverous flesh, livid and lined, gleamed its two eyes, partly closed, but one more so than the other, and they seemed to wink, as if to say:

"For a long time, while I lay waiting there in my box, I meditated some ghastly surprise for you, and at last you have come; you are in my power, and here it is."

Well, for those who have eyes to see, the face of their Kaiser is as shocking as that mask, hidden away in the old temple over there; it matters not in what kind of helmet, more or less savage in design, he may choose to trick himself out, whether it have a spike or a death's head. In all the years during which the terrible expression of this man has haunted me, I not only shared the presentiment common to everyone else that he was "meditating some surprise for us," but I had a foreboding that his plot would be laid with diabolical wickedness and would prove more terrible than all the crimes of old, uncivilised times. And I said to myself:

"It is of vital importance for the safeguard of humanity to kill that thing."

Indeed he should have been killed, the hyena slain, before his latent rabidness had completely developed, or at least he should have been chained up, muzzled, imprisoned behind close set and solid bars.

What could have possessed the anarchists, to whom such an opportunity presented itself of redeeming their character, of deserving the gratitude of the world, what could have possessed them? When there is question of killing a sovereign they attempt the life of the charming young King of Spain. From the Austrian court, which held a far more suitable victim, they select and stab the mysterious and lovely Empress, who never harmed a soul. And of the quartet of kings in the Balkans, their choice fell upon the King of Greece, when there was that monster Coburg close at hand, an opportunity truly unique.

Their Kaiser, their unspeakable, Protean Kaiser, whenever it seems that everything possible has been said about him, bewilders one by breaking out in some new direction which no one could ever have foreseen. After his almost doltish obstinacy in persistently posing his Germany as the victim who was attacked, in spite of most blinding evidence to the contrary, most formal written proofs, most crushing confessions which escaped the lips of his accomplices, did he not just recently feel a need to "swear before God" that his conscience was pure and that he had not wished for war? Before what God? Obviously before his own, "his old God," proper to himself, whom in private he must assuredly call, "my old Beelzebub." What excellent taste, moreover, to couple that epithet "old" with such a name!

This Kaiser of theirs seems to have received from his old Beelzebub not only a mission to spread abroad the uttermost mourning, to cause the most abundant outpouring of blood and tears, but also a mission to shoot down all forms of beauty, all religious memorials; a mission to profane everything, defile everything, and disfigure everything that he should fail to destroy. He has succeeded even in bringing dishonour on science, by degrading it to play the part of accomplice in his crimes. Moreover it is not merely that this war of his, this war which he forced upon us with such damnable deliberation, will have been a thousand times more destructive of human life than all the wars of the past collectively, but he must needs likewise attack with vindictive fury, he and his rabble of followers, all those treasures of art which should have remained an inviolable heritage of civilised Europe. And if ever he had succeeded in realising his dream of morbid vanity and becoming absolute tyrant of the world, not by means of explosives and scrap-iron alone would he have achieved the ruin of all art, but through the incurably bad taste of his Germany. It is sufficient to have visited Berlin, the capital city of pinchbeck, of the gilded decorations of the parvenu, to form an idea of what our towns would have become. And with a shudder one contemplates the rapid and final decadence of those wonderful Eastern towns, Stamboul, Damascus, Bagdad, upon the day when they should submit to his law.

This unspeakable Kaiser of theirs, how

cunningly sometimes he adds to dishonour a touch of the grotesque. For instance, did he not lately offer as a pledge to that insignificant King of Greece his word of a Hohenzollern? The day after the violation of Belgium to dare to offer his word was admirable enough, but to add that his word was that of a Hohenzollern, what a happy conceit! Is it the result of dense unconsciousness or of the insolent irony with which he regards his timid brother-in-law, at whose little army, on the occasion of a visit to Athens, he scoffed so disdainfully? Who that has some slight tincture of history is ignorant of the fact that during the five hundred years of its notoriety the accursed line of the Hohenzollern has never produced anything but shameless liars, kites that prey on flesh. As early as 1762 did not the great Empress Maria Theresa write of them in these terms:

"All the world knows what value to attach to the King of Prussia and his word. There is no sovereign in Europe who has not suffered from his perfidy. And such a king as this would impose himself upon Germany as dictator and protector! Under a despotism which repudiates every principle, the Prussian monarchy will one day be the source of infinite calamity, not only to Germany, but likewise to the whole of Europe."

Unhappy King of Greece, who approached too near to the glare of the Gorgon, and lies to-day annihilated almost by its baleful influence! Should not his example be as much an object lesson—though without the heroism and the glory—for sovereigns of neutral nations who have still been spared, as the examples of the King of Belgium and the King of Serbia?

Their Kaiser, whose mere glance is ominous of death, baffles reason and common sense. The morbid degeneracy of his brain is undeniable, and yet in certain respects it is nevertheless a brain excellently ordered for planning evil, and it has made a special study of the art of slaughter. For the honour of humanity let us grant that he is mad, as a certain prince of Saxony has just publicly declared.

Agreed; he is mad. His case may actually be classified as teratological, and in any other country but Germany this war of his would have resulted for him in a strait-waistcoat and a cell. But alas for Europe! the accident of his birth has made him Kaiser of the one nation capable of tolerating him and of obeying him—a people cruel by nature and rendered ferocious by civilisation, as Goethe avers; a people of infinite stupidity, as Schopenhauer confesses in his last solemn testament.

In some respects this infinite stupidity

he himself shares. Otherwise would he have failed so irremediably in his first outset in 1914 as to imagine up to the very last moment that England would not stir, even in face of Belgium's great sacrifice.[1] And is there not at least as much folly as ferocity in his massacres of civilians, his torpedoing of ships belonging to neutral countries, his outrages in America, his Zeppelins, his asphyxiating gas; all those odious crimes which he personally insti-

[1] In addition to a thousand other widely known examples of his shameless knavery, I record another instance, which, moreover, may easily be verified; an instance perhaps not yet sufficiently widely published. Be it known to everyone that on August 2nd, 1914, on the very eve of the violation of Belgium, when the German Army was already massed on the frontier and all the orders had been given for the attack the next day, King Albert called upon the Kaiser for an explanation. The Kaiser replied officially through his diplomatists:

"The Belgians have no cause for alarm. I have not the slightest intention of repudiating my signature."

gated, and which have had merely the result of concentrating upon himself and his German Empire universal hatred and disgust?

After forty years of feverish preparation, with such formidable resources at his disposal, shrinking from no measures however atrocious and vile, trammelled by no law of humanity, by no pang of conscience, to wallow thus in blood, and yet after all to achieve nothing but failure—there is no other explanation possible; some essential quality must be lacking in his murderous brain. And the nation must indeed be German in character still to suffer itself to be led onwards to its downfall by an unbalanced lunatic responsible for such blunders. They are led onwards to downfall and butchery. And is there never a limit to the sheepish submission of a people who at this very moment are suffering themselves to be slaughtered like mere cattle in attacks directed with imbecile fury by a microcephalous youth, equally devoid of intelligence and soul?

II

Ferdinand of Coburg

But recently it would have seemed an impossible wager to undertake to find an even more abominable monster than their Kaiser and their Crown Prince. Nevertheless the wager has been made and won; this Coburg has been found.

And to think that in his time he aroused the enthusiasm of the majority of our women of France! About the year 1913, when I alone was beginning to nail him to the pillory, they were exalting his name and flaunting his colours. "Paladin of the Cross"—as such he was popularly known among us. Oh, a sincere paladin he was, to be sure, wearing the scapular, steeped in Masses, after the fashion of

Louis XI., yet one fine morning secretly forcing apostasy upon his son. Moreover we know that to-day, for our entertainment, he is making preparations for a second comedy of conversion to the Catholic faith, which he recently renounced for political reasons, and over there he will find priests ready to bless the operation and to keep a straight face the while.

He, too, has a Gorgon's head, and his face, like the Kaiser's, is marked with the stigmata of knavery and crime. Twenty-five years ago, at the railway station of Sofia, when for the first time I came under the malevolent glance of his small eyes, I felt my nerves vibrate with that shudder of disgust which is an instinctive warning of the proximity of a monster, and I asked:

"Who is that vampire?"

Someone replied in a low, apprehensive voice:

"It is our prince; you should bow to him."

Ah, no indeed; not that!

In private life this man has proved himself a cowardly assassin, committing his murders from a safe distance, for he prudently crossed the border whenever his executioner had "work to do" by his orders. And then, as soon as any particular headsman threatened to compromise him he would take effective steps to cripple him.[1]

And this man, too, offers up prayers in imitation of that other. Recently, when there was a hope that his great accomplice was at last about to die of the hereditary taint in his blood, he knelt for a long time between two rows of Germans, convoked as audience, to plead with heaven for his recovery—a monster praying on behalf of another monster—and he arose, steeped in divine grace, and said to the audience:

"I have never before prayed so fervently."

---

[1] Panitza, Stambouloff, etc.

Those heavy-witted Boches, for whose benefit these apish antics were performed, were even they able to restrain their wild laughter? In political life, likewise, he is an assassin, attempting the life of nations. After his first foul act of treason against Serbia, his former ally, whom he took in the rear without any declaration of war, he endeavoured, it will be remembered, to throw upon his ministers the blame of a crime which was threatening to turn out badly. And again without warning he deals another traitorous blow to the same race of heroes, already overwhelmed by immense hordes of barbarians, like a highwayman who, under pretence of helping, comes from behind to give the finishing stroke to a man already at grips with a band of robbers.

Poor little Serbia, now grown great and sublime! Lately, in my first moments of indignation at the report that reached me of deeds of horror perpetrated in Thrace and Macedonia, I had accused her undeservedly of sharing in the guilt. Once again in these pages I tender her with all my heart my *amende honorable*.

If Germany's *entente* with Turkey was so little capable of being accomplished unassisted that it was found necessary to have recourse to the "suicide" of the hereditary prince, the *entente* with Bulgaria was made spontaneously. *Their* Kaiser and this scion of the Coburgs, who emulates him, and is, as it were, his duplicate in miniature, found each other fatally easy to understand. That such sympathy was likely to exist between them might have been gathered from a mere comparison of the two faces, each bearing the same expression of beasts that prowl in the night. How was it that our diplomatists, accredited to the little court of Sofia, suspected nothing nearly twenty months ago, when the treaty of brigandage was signed in secret? And to-day, until one devours the other, behold them united, these two beings, the refuse of humanity, compared with whom the foulest, most hardened offenders, who drag a cannon-ball along in a convict's prison, seem to have committed nothing but harmless and trifling offences.

Arouse yourselves, then, neutral nations, great and small, who still fail to realise that had it not been for us your turn would have come to be trampled underfoot like Belgium, like Serbia and Montenegro only yesterday! The world will not breathe freely until these ultimate barbarians have been completely crushed; how is it that you have not felt this? What else can be necessary to open your eyes? If it is not enough for you to witness in our country all the ruin inflicted on us of set purpose and to no useful end, to read a vast number of irrefutable testimonies of furi-

WAR 317

ous massacres which spared not even our little children; if all this is not enough look nearer home, look at the insolent irony with which this predatory race brings pressure to bear upon you, look at all the outrages, done audaciously or by stealth, which have already been committed on the other side of the ocean. Or again, if indeed you are blind to that which goes on around you, at least survey briefly all the writings, during centuries, of their men of letters, their "great men." You will be horrified to discover on every page the most barefaced apology for violence, rapine, and crime. Thus you will establish the fact that all the horror with which Europe is inundated to-day was contained from the beginning in embryo there in German brains, and, moreover, that no other race on earth would have dared to denounce itself with such cynical insensibility. And you, priests or monks, belonging to the clergy of a neighbouring country, who reproach us with impiety and are the blindest of men in proselytising for our enemies, turn over a few pages of the official manifesto addressed to the Belgian bishops, and tell us what to think of the soul of a people who continually take in vain the name of the "All Highest" in their burlesque prayers, and then make furious attacks on all the sanctuaries of religion, cathedrals, or humble village churches, overthrowing the crucifixes and massacring the priests. Is it logically possible for anyone, not of their accursed race, to love the Germans? That a nation may remain neutral I can understand, but only from fear, or from lack of due preparation, or perhaps, without realising it, for the lure of a certain momentary gain, through a little mistaken and shortsighted selfishness. Oh, doubtless it is a terrible thing to hurl oneself into such a fray! Yet neutrality, hesitation even, become worse than dangerous mistakes; they are already almost crimes.

An insane scoundrel dreamed of forcing upon us all the ways of two thousand years ago, the degrading serfdom of ancient days, the dark ages of old; he plotted to bring about for his own profit a general bankruptcy of progress, liberty, human thought, and after us, you, you neutral nations, were designated as sacrifices to his insatiable, ogreish appetite. At least help us a little to bring to a more rapid conclusion this orgy of robbery, destruction, massacres, and bloodshed. Enough, let us awaken from this nightmare! Enough, let the whole world arise! Whosoever holds back to-day, will he not be ashamed to keep his place in the sun of victory and peace when it once more shines upon us? And we, when at last we have laid low the rabid hyena, after pouring out our blood in streams, should we not almost have a right to say, with our weapons still in our hands:

"You neutral nations, who will profit by the deliverance, having taken no part in the struggle, the least you can do is to repay us in some measure with your territory or with your gold?"

Oh, everywhere let the tocsin clang, a full peal, ringing from end to end of the earth; let the supreme alarm ring out, and let the drums of all the armies roll the charge! And down with the German Beast!